Derek C. Hutchinson's

Guide to Expedition Kayaking on Sea and Open Water

"There are few books that offer as much information as this one. . . . You can kayak without knowing this information, but going beyond the recreational stage is made much easier after reading *Sea Kayaking*."

—*Canoe & Kayak*

"Hutchinson stresses that neither age nor sex is a barrier in this sport, but planning and careful preparation are all-important. His considerable experience, the clear illustrations, and interesting passages from early kayak explorers' texts, along with a dry wit and a very personal style of writing, make this a pleasure to read."

—*Library Journal*

"If you want someone to trust for serious sea kayaking advice, Derek Hutchinson is your man."

—*River Runner*

Derek C. Hutchinson's

Guide to
EXPEDITION KAYAKING
on Sea and Open Water

Third Edition

by

Derek C. Hutchinson

An East Woods Book

The Globe Pequot Press

Old Saybrook, Connecticut

Library of Congress Cataloging-in-Publication Data

Hutchinson, Derek C.
   [Guide to Expedition kayaking]
   Derek C. Hutchinson's guide to expedition kayaking : on sea and open water / by Derek C. Hutchinson.—3rd ed.
        p.   cm.
   Rev. ed. of : Derek C. Hutchinson's guide to sea kayaking. 2nd ed. c 1990.
   Includes index.
   ISBN 1-56440-721-7
   1. Sea kayaking. I. Hutchinson, Derek C. Guide to sea kayaking. II. Title.
   GV788.5.H87 1995   95-15108
   797.1'224—dc20   CIP

Manufactured in the United States of America
Third Edition/Second Printing

To Alistair Wilson, Tom Caskey, Chris Jowsey, and George Peck—
true friends and my companions in search of the
killer whales of Prince William Sound, Alaska.

And to all those who have chosen to venture upon
the sea in the most beautiful of all solo craft—
the Hunter's Boat or kayak of the Arctic.

Contents

Acknowledgments

I am fortunate to number among my friends those whom I would consider to be the best in the world of the men and women who paddle the kayak on the open sea. It has been through their stories and my own experiences that I have been able to write this book. My thanks to Frank Goodman for his invaluable help, especially on the subject of plastic sea kayaks, and to Chris Jowsey, Martin Meling, Alan Byde, and Clive Hutchinson. I am also indebted to Larry Willis of Florida for his alligator noises; Molly Jones, mother of the late Dr. Mike Jones; Mike Clark of *Canoeing* magazine; Derek Bamforth of Pacific Canoe Base, Victoria, British Columbia; Gary and Mercia Sixta of the Vancouver Kayak Club; Will Nordby of San Francisco; Matt Broze of the Washington Kayak Club; Steve Sinclair of Force 10, Elk, California; Werner Furrer, kayak designer of Washington State; Robert Licht of Sea Trek Ocean Kayaking Center, Sausalito, California; and Gary Birnham of Sydney, Australia.

A big thank you must go to Mary Padwick, who suffered the job of correcting, organizing, and typing my scrambled manuscript, and to Ron Leamon, who undertook the job of editing the whole affair. Thanks also to Dave (Dancingbear) Hunsaker of Juneau, Alaska, for making me see the need for this book.

I am also grateful for the facilities offered by the Literary and Philosophical Society of Newcastle-upon-Tyne.

And thank you to the thief who ransacked my car and stole my briefcase, but left the separate sheets of this manuscript spread around among the trees of a nearby park—in the rain.

Acknowledgments to the Third Edition

For their contributions to this third edition, I would like to thank the following: Didier Plouhinic, Barry Howell, Martin Meling, Linda Legg, Dr. Michael Watts, Kevin Danforth, Howard Jeffs, Scott Williams, Will Nordby, Dr. Margaret Taylor, Kevin Mansell, Bill Moore, Brian Melville, and Geoff Good, Director of Coaching of the British Canoe Union.

The tests and awards (Appendixes I, II, and III) are reproduced by courtesy of the British Canoe Union.

INTRODUCTION

I stood on a green velvet lawn and held the kayak paddle tightly in my clenched hands. It was the spring of 1963, and suitably spaced around me were about ten other individuals all clutching their paddles tightly. We faced in the same direction, and the object of our attention was an older, rather rounded gentleman who also held a paddle. He had demonstrated the correct method of holding and handling this strange piece of equipment. We in turn tried to copy his movements. Paddles flailed through the air and every now and again there would be a loud clack as paddle collided with paddle. I decided that I was completely uncoordinated but at least I felt some comfort when I looked at what appeared to be a host of ruptured windmills.

It was a beautiful Saturday morning, however, and the sun was shining. My Education Authority had already held a number of "taster" courses in outdoor education for teachers in their service. A few of us at the school where I taught felt that the potential entertainment value of these courses was too good to be ignored, so we had given them our wholehearted support. The "Introduction to Camping" weekend had been fun, but as far as the "Introduction to Rock Climbing" was concerned, I had decided that discretion was the better part of valor. I am terrified of heights and I felt that the sight of a grown man crying

might have upset the weekend for everyone else. I had decided to save myself for the kayaking weekend on the grounds that I liked water and that if I capsized, I would not have far to fall.

Around us on the lawn lay kayaks of varying shapes and sizes. I still felt demoralized by my apparent lack of coordination, and I was relieved when we were asked to follow our instructor over to a small outdoor swimming pool. This worthy man got into one of the kayaks with an ease that amazed me and proceeded to demonstrate the forward paddling stroke on the water. He showed us how to stop the boat and also how to paddle backward. To finish off, he pointed out to the onlookers that it was vital that everyone should be able to vacate the kayak easily in the event of a capsize. He demonstrated this to his now rather nervous audience by suddenly turning his boat upside down, waiting for about three seconds, then exiting from the cockpit. I was horrified, but he surfaced unhurriedly, with a beaming face. Now it was our turn, he announced, and suddenly I felt ill.

One by one my associates capsized beneath the clear blue water, and more and more I wished that I had not come on what had turned out to be a masochistic if not suicidal weekend. Then it was my turn. It was obvious to any fool that the cockpit was far too small and that I would stick fast. I did not relish the thought of a claustrophobic, choking death at the hands of this madman—and said so. We talked, he persuaded, and I capsized. Suddenly I was standing up to my waist in water; miraculously, I had survived. I don't even remember leaving the cockpit and yet it had worried me sick. I decided there was nothing to it and I was all attention when our instructor announced that he was going to give us a demonstration of handling techniques that would be something for us to aim for.

I don't know what I expected to see, but as before, he entered the kayak with an easy familiarity. He pulled a spray cover over the cockpit coaming and it was as if he had, by some freak of evolution, suddenly grown a kayak where his legs should have been. The boat became an extension of his body.

To say that it was a delight to watch this man move his kayak around in this tiny pool would be an understatement. He handled and held his paddle as gently as some fairy queen would hold her wand, and the ballet he performed with that boat would have done credit to *Swan Lake*. Every movement was controlled, every lean was the picture of grace. On the face of this artist—and he was an artist—was a look of utter contentment. A glance around at the faces of the other onlookers told me that they also were enthralled. I had arrived at this course rather bored and indifferent, but this man had held me spellbound. His name was Alan Byde and he was a senior coach with the British Canoe Union. This was the highest pinnacle a man could reach and I decided that I wanted to be like him. That first capsize seems a lifetime ago, but the same Alan, who is now my friend, would be the first to admit that my life has never been quite the same since.

Ocean kayaking is a sport in which age and sex are not barriers, and I cannot think of many physical activities that can be done equally well by men and women between the ages of eighteen and eighty all in the same group. Paddling a kayak is also a very personal thing. Once secure inside the cockpit and

snug on the molded bucket seat, it soon becomes obvious to the occupant that it is a boat that is worn rather than sat in. Every mood and movement of the sea is transmitted through the hull of the kayak to the paddler's nervous system. In this way a union is built up between the paddler and the sea.

The challenge of the ocean kayak is more than a physical one, and I've especially found the navigational aspects of the sport mentally stimulating. Because of the boat's obvious restrictions, any navigation has to go back to basics. Because the paddler can have no sextant to locate his position or log to gauge his speed, he has to rely solely on his compass, a chart, and a good memory. I remember as if it were yesterday the days of waiting prior to my second attempt to make a crossing of the North Sea. Every evening we would get out the chart and plan the long trip, anticipating good weather for the following day. With nervous apprehension, we finally set off at 6:30 A.M. on a morning early in June. We knew that the fast tidal streams change direction every six hours and that the mainlands of England and Belgium in the area of our crossing were below sea level. This would mean that we would have no land upon which to fix our eyes. Thirty-one hours later, to our relief and satisfaction, we landed exactly where we had intended—on the beach at Ostend.

Even the shortest journeys by kayak are true voyages of discovery. It may be along a familiar bit of tree-lined coast or in and out of the jetties and moorings of some seaport town or city. Wherever it may be, you will see the world, your companions, and yourself from a completely different angle; and if you are like me, it will be an experience that never becomes jaded. For those who are unable to travel far from their homes, the same piece of water can be paddled over many times—the backdrop may remain the same, but the stage is always different.

I have written this book so that it is not simply a text about how to kayak. Rather, it is a book on how to kayak in such a way as to live to kayak another day. In it I have attempted to provide enough information to stimulate the experienced paddler and to help those who are becoming proficient to overcome many of the problems and situations they may be faced with. I have assumed a certain level of expertise on the part of the reader and have not described all the basic techniques and maneuvers.

Most of your kayaking may be done as part of coastal touring or as island-hopping trips in areas familiar to you. Once in a while, however, you may be driven by a mixture of curiosity and a sense of adventure to transport your seaworthy little boat to wild, faraway, and unfamiliar coastlines. There you will find that just about anything can happen and usually does. That is why this book is filled with facts that may not solve the problem, but at least it ensures that the problem itself will not come as a great surprise.

No sport stands still, and the world of expedition kayaking is no exception. I have tried to find the time between my own paddling adventures to update this little volume. Since the book was first published, a number of problems have come to notice. I had been going to say "new" problems, but of course the problems are as old as the hills. It is just that the kayak has given us the opportunity to face them firsthand.

While paddling along one of Florida's dreamy, quiet waterways, I surprised an alligator. Did I say *I* surprised the alligator? Believe that if you will! The creature took off from the small hidden beach at high speed. It must have been at least 18 feet long—well, all right, perhaps it *was* only 8 feet long, but then the sun was in my eyes! That alligator is now much wiser. It now knows, for instance, that Caucasians can change color from pink to white in a matter of seconds without the use of dyes or bleaches. Later the same year, a tick strolled along my foredeck and attempted to savage me. Fear of Lyme disease gave me the strength to fight it off with my paddle, and I realized it was just something else for the global kayaker to think about. Apart from the problems posed by alligators and deer ticks, I felt the need to mention the danger of shark attack.

The chapter dealing with waves has also been expanded, and a movement diagram for the screw roll should make it easier for those who wish to teach themselves this technique. Finally, I decided that plastic sea kayaks also deserved a place in the new edition.

With this book, as with previous editions, I have assumed a certain level of skill on the part of the reader. This new edition has been expanded in almost every direction and in keeping with the book's general bias, I felt that it should now be known as my *Guide to Expedition Kayaking on Sea and Open Water.* I have removed anything I thought was outdated. The other material has been brought into line with current thinking and practice, and the whole book is now much enlarged with several new sections. This edition features many new illustrations, both diagrams and photographs.

I have further explored the subject of double kayaks. I have also introduced kayak sailing as an option for those who wish to experiment. The book contains much additional information for expedition paddlers and leaders. I felt that I should give the prospective camper some advice, as well as much more information, regarding hazardous wildlife. I describe a new way to remove fish hooks and also a means of protection against lightning. (In 1994 there were more people struck by lightning in Florida than at any other time in the state's history—and, unfortunately, this included two kayakers.)

Just as the previous edition was written to be a companion book to *Sea Canoeing,* so this new *Guide to Expedition Kayaking* is the companion book, for intermediate and advanced kayakers, to *The Complete Book of Sea Kayaking.*

THE KAYAK

The Beginnings

It was the Eskimo's kayak that started it all, of course. But the early explorers who gazed upon this strange little boat of driftwood and skin probably never dreamed it would later be adapted and used for recreational purposes and on the oceans of the world. Those early explorers were impressed—even awed—by the kayak and the skills displayed by the original kayakers, and today's paddlers can find instruction as well as entertainment in the writings of Fridtjof Nansen, David Crantz, and others. Reading Nansen's detailed description of a century ago, one is struck by the Eskimo's ingenuity in utilizing available materials:

It has an internal framework of wood. This, of which the reader can, I hope, form some conception from the accompanying drawing, was formerly always made of driftwood, usually of the white wood, which is the lightest [fig. 1-1]. For the ribs, osiers were sometimes used, from willow bushes which are found growing far up the fiords. In later days they have got into the habit of buying European boards of spruce and Scotch fir in the west coast colonies, although driftwood is still considered preferable . . . on account of its lightness.

This framework is covered externally with skins, as a rule with the skin of the saddleback seal *(Phoca groenlandica),* or of the bladder-nose or hood seal *(Cystophora cristata).* The latter is not so durable or so water-tight as the former; but the skin of a young bladder-nose, in which the pores are not yet very large, is considered good enough. . . . the skin of the bearded seal *(Phoca barbata)* . . . is reckoned the best and strongest. . . . the skin of the great ringed seal *(Phoca toetida)* is also used. . . .

. . . The preparation of the skins, and the sewing and stretching them on the kaiak, belongs to the women's department; it is not very easy work, and woe to them if the skin sits badly or is too slack. They feel it a great disgrace.

In the middle of the kaiak's deck there is a hole just large enough to enable a man to get his legs through it and to sit down; his thighs almost entirely fill the aperture. Thus it takes a good deal of practice before one can slip into or out of the kaiak with any sort of ease. The hole is surrounded by the kaiak-ring, which consists of a hoop of wood. It stands a little more than an inch (3 or 3½ centimeters) above the kaiak's deck, and the waterproof jacket, as we shall presently see, is drawn over it. At the spot where the rower sits, pieces of old kaiak skin are laid in the bottom

1-1. This is an Eskimo kayak and its frame. The letter on the original illustration indicates placement of hunting weapons. (From Fidtjof Nansen, *Eskimo Life* [London, 1983], p. 44.)

A Greenlander in his kajak is indeed an object of wonder and delight, and his sable sea dress, shining with rows of white bone buttons, gives him a splendid appearance. He rows with extreme celerity in this boat. . . . He dreads no storm: as long as a ship can carry its top-sail, he braves the mountainous billows, darting over them like a bird, and even when completely buried in the waves, he soon re-appears skimming along the surface. If a breaker threatens to overset him, he supports himself in an erect position by his oar, or if he is actually upset, he restores himself to his balance by one swing of his paddle. But if he loses the oar, it is certain death, unless speedy succour be at hand.

Some Europeans have by dint of application attained sufficient command of the kajak for a calm-weather voyage; but they seldom venture to fish in it, and are totally helpless in dangerous situations. The Greenlanders possess in the management of this vessel, a dexterity peculiar to themselves, which excites a fearful interest in the spectator. . . . (David Crantz, History of Greenland: Including an Account of the Mission Carried on by the Bretheren of That Country, *2 vols. [London: Longman, Hurst, Rees, Orme, and Brown, 1820], 1:139–40.)*

over the ribs, with a piece of bearskin or other fur to make the seat softer.

As a rule, each hunter makes his kaiak for himself, and it is fitted to the man's size just like a garment. The bottom of the kaiak is pretty flat, sloping to a very obtuse angle (probably about 140°) in the middle. The kaiak narrows evenly in, both fore and aft, and comes to a point at both ends. It has no keel, but its underpart at both ends is generally provided with bone flanges, for the most part of whale-rib, designed to save the skin from being ripped up by drift-ice, or by stones when the kaiak is beached. Both points are commonly provided with knobs of bone, partly for ornament, partly for protection as well.

Across the deck, in front of the kaiak-ring, six thongs are usually fastened, and from three to five behind the rower. Under these thongs weapons and implements are inserted, so that they lie safe and handy for use. (Fridtjof Nansen, *Eskimo Life*, trans. William Archer [London: Longmans, Green, and Co. 1893], pp. 44–45.)

Although Nansen writes as if there were only one design, Eskimo kayak designs varied considerably from place to place (see fig. 1-2). Differences in design are easy to understand when the kayaks were from areas separated by considerable distance, but designs from the same area often had marked differences as well. These variations—

West Greenland
(18' × 18")

Northwest Alaska
(17' × 18")

Mackenzie Delta, Canada
(16' × 19")

Unalaska, Aleutian Islands
(18' × 20")

Unalaska, Aleutian Islands
(18' × 20")

1-2 Inuit and Aleut skin boats that have influenced modern sea kayak design

and were built with long journeys in mind. The type of sea and weather conditions to be faced also influenced design. Kayaks intended for use in sheltered fjords tended to be low in the water with little freeboard. Boats that had to cope with rough seas often had steeply pitched decks.

These uses for the kayak suggest how important the kayak was to the Eskimos. Indeed, it was an almost indispensable part of their way of life. But that way of life has passed now, and the skin boats are nearly gone. Aleuts and Inuits today go about their business in dories with outboard motors. I like to think, though, that in modern replicas of the "hunter's boat" we can keep the skills and some of the original spirit alive.

The Modern Sea Kayak

Since the latter part of the nineteenth century, when John Macgregor brought his heavy Rob Roy canoe to the attention of the public, numerous craft supposedly modeled upon native North American and Arctic boats have been built. Many of these were strange looking indeed, and few resembled even the clumsiest of the original skin boats.

In the early 1960s the advent of fiberglass to the boating scene gave designers a medium in which graceful curves were easier to reproduce. No longer were they restricted by the limitations of lath and fabric. The result was the appearance over the next decade of a number of sea kayaks that were aesthetically pleasing and clearly influenced by the Arctic skin boats. It is only since the beginning of the 1970s that the real potential of the sea kayak has been realized.

At present in Britain there are five or six leading sea kayak designs, and all are based on the styles of the original skin boats of North America and the Arctic. If the reader of these pages detects a preference on my part for these boats, it is

some subtle and some not so subtle—were due to a number of factors. The function of the kayak was a primary consideration in the design. Some were designed to carry heavy loads and consequently had a lot of freeboard. Others were designed to be sleek and fast for hunting. Still others were designed to carry more than one person

1-3. This is a model of a Kotzebue kayak. The tiny boat is covered with walrus intestine. (Photo courtesy Clive Hutchinson)

because they and a few others being produced in Europe have been proved internationally in a variety of rough water conditions.

In contrast, the use in modern-day North America of the one-person kayak is still in its embryonic stage. (Credit must go to the North Americans for pioneering the use of the two-person, or double, kayak on the open sea, for making seaworthy double kayaks, and for proving them in a variety of conditions.) During the last few years the popularity of the one-person kayak has increased dramatically in North America, and numerous one-person kayak designs have appeared on the market to keep pace with the demand. Many of these kayaks have been designed to cope with sea conditions that can be found only in certain areas, while others have had no time to be tested and proved in the variety of conditions necessary to give the kayaks universal appeal.

Challenges of Kayak Design

In all fairness it must be said that anyone who designs kayaks for use on the open sea is faced with a number of complex and frustrating problems. To satisfy discerning paddlers, the finished masterpiece must be light enough for anyone to toss onto a vehicle, yet strong and heavy enough to withstand the pressures and batterings of rough usage. A kayak must also run straight at all times—even in the most trying conditions—yet turn easily when the need arises. It must be stable enough to give the timid confidence, but narrow enough to make rolling an untroubled maneuver. The hull must be voluminous enough to accommodate a mountain of equipment, but the amount of freeboard must be kept to a minimum. The seat should be comfortable and give good support for many hours, and it must also be in the correct position so that the occupant trims the boat when it is paddled. High seats breed high speeds and instability. Low seats give stability, but they can also provide the paddler with bruised and wet elbows and skinned knuckles.

Designers face all these tantalizing dilemmas in a variety of ways with the end result that there is no such thing as a perfect sea kayak. All are a compromise in one way or another, and when making a decision as to which one to buy, a paddler or potential paddler must use his own judgment, tempered by the advice of more experienced friends and as many "dry runs" in different boats as he can manage. My own advice, based on many years as a sea kayaker and designer of sea kayaks, is presented in the sections that follow.

Hull Shape

A good hull shape is, of course, vital for sustained high speeds. The best hulls are from 21 to 24 inches wide and 15 to 17 feet long and are designed with a bottom shape that runs straight and tracks well even in a quartering sea aft. Any turning or correcting is done by leaning the kayak over onto its broadest section amidships and sweeping the paddle blade out far enough on the forward paddle stroke to bring the boat back around onto its correct heading.

An important factor governing speed in choppy conditions is the shape of the bow. Bow shapes can be of two designs: the very buoyant design that rides over normal-sized oncoming waves or one designed to slice and not plunge through the waves. The former works well except when seas are very steep and cause the bow to plunge and displace the water violently sideways. The displaced water then falls back and collides on the foredeck. The resulting clapotis (collision of waves)—a couple of feet from the bow—hits the forward-moving paddler in the face.

The slicing bow, on the other hand, cuts through the wave, throwing very little water sideways, and has a foredeck shaped to allow the bow to rise cleanly from the wave. A good slicing bow does not work solely through lack of buoyancy at the fore-end, as this will cause the kayak to submarine, but rather by careful planning and design.

No matter how designed, the bow should be fine (or narrow) enough to promote a smooth laminar flow of water over the forepart of the hull. The stern is also very important. This, too, should be fine, thereby minimizing any drag brought about by water separation. The stern also should be high enough to balance any windage the bow might receive and to prevent the otherwise good feature of a powerful bow from being blown downwind.

Wood and fabric folding boats, which are wide and flat-bottomed, are naturally very stable on flat water. Unfortunately, they tend to follow the angle of the water beneath them—rather disconcerting if the seas are steep. When paddling these boats in rough seas or breaking waves, most kayakers prefer to meet the seas head on because the design precludes any techniques other than those of a very basic kind. For this reason I consider these boats to belong to a branch of our sport apart from that of the modern fiberglass ocean kayak.

Cockpits

In the modern kayak, the coastlines for which designs have been intended have had a major impact on cockpit size. The coastline of Great Britain is virtually unprotected and open to large swells and sudden storms. Because of this, British designers have made their cockpits comparable in size to those of whitewater boats. Cockpits any smaller than this depend on the relative heights of the fore- and reardecks. Some of the skin boats from Greenland and Labrador, for example, have foredecks higher than the reardecks. The difference in height between the fore- and reardecks makes entry (and exit) quite easy; to enter one simply has to sit on the reardeck and slide into the cockpit with the legs straight.

Many of the boats designed in North America, in contrast, have fore- and reardecks of the same height (or nearly the same height). Because of this, the cockpit openings are, of necessity, very large. Many of these boats are intended for paddlers who wish to explore relatively protected coastlines. In the Pacific Northwest, for example, the generally contorted coastline that extends from Puget Sound to Glacier Bay, Alaska, has thousands of miles of islands, and deep fjords. A lifetime could be spent paddling this coastline without ever having to face the rigors and stresses of the open sea. In such cases, kayaks with large cockpits are perhaps adequate.

On the other hand, if one wishes to paddle unprotected coastlines or to be safe in the event of sudden violent storms, kayaks with large cockpits are, in my considered opinion, risky. Ideally, the ocean paddler should be supported in much the same way as the river paddler; she should have support at the feet, knees, thighs, and seat. In a large cockpit it is often impossible to brace the knees. This deficiency is sometimes compounded by a poorly designed and loosely fitting seat, one that resembles a tiny armchair and offers no support to the thighs. Paddlers who own such boats can to an extent compensate by the addition of specially cut pieces of closed-cell foam carefully positioned and glued in place with contact cement.

Some cockpits are so large that the designers have provided sliding seats. The idea is to allow the paddler to trim the boat by sliding his weight back and forth. That the trim can be altered is no doubt true, but it can be argued that it is more advantageous to have a secure seat in a well-planned position that enables the paddler to brace himself and apply good technique to his corrective paddling strokes.

Over the last few years it has been comforting to see the inclusion of many more seaworthy features in U.S. designs. I was pleased to see that Brian Henry of Current Designs finally succumbed to my persuasion and now builds most of his kayaks with recessed deck fittings. This affords less damage to knuckles, spray skirts, and waterproof bags. A number of designers have also given their attention to the lack of leg support in large cockpits. One solution has been to alter the shape of the coaming to provide knee support.

To allow the spray cover to fit snugly but safely, the cockpit coaming should be at least three-fourths inches wide and have sufficient clearance to allow a person's fingers to run around between it and the deck without jamming. The spray cover should fit tightly around the cockpit coaming and be in good condition. Because the cover fits tightly, the release strap should be secure and efficient. One foolproof method is to affix with fiberglass a piece of webbing tape (approximately one foot long) underneath the deck just in front of the cockpit. Fit a loop or toggle to the end and lead this out of the cockpit and onto the top of the deck. No matter how tight the spray cover, it will come off with one pull without damage. After all, it is no good wrenching hard on a release strap only to have the strap pull off with the spray

cover still in place. Did I say foolproof? Do not forget to place the release straps on the *outside* before putting on the spray-cover.

Hatches and Bulkheads

The greatest innovation in ocean kayak design in recent years has been the introduction of watertight hatches and bulkheads. (See fig. 1-4; hatches are also discussed below, under Deck Layout.) Equipment can be kept dry at all times, and the boat is virtually unsinkable. Any hatch that allows entry into the interior of a kayak should be watertight and designed so that it cannot be knocked off or displaced during deep-water rescues or when breaking seas crash across the deck. Some kayaks, which manufacturers claim are designed for the ocean, exhibit hatches that are held in place by flimsy turn buttons, thin shock cord, or snap clips that would be better employed on a cheap suitcase than on an ocean-going craft. A kayak fitted in this manner should be viewed with suspicion. There is nothing wrong with a large hatch opening, so long as it remains watertight.

A small bilge pump can be fitted where it will not interfere with normal paddling, but most manufacturers place them on the reardeck just aft of the cockpit on either the left- or right-hand side. Also on the market is an excellent foot-operated pump that is fixed to the footrest (the Lendal foot pump, fig. 1-5). Although this does not have the same discharge volume as the hand-operated version, it can be used without any interruption of the paddle stroke. I prefer to have both fitted just to be on the safe side.

Hull Strength and Weight

The decks of sea kayaks should be strong enough to support deep-water rescues or the weight of a distressed comrade if the need arises. Such stressful situations will soon reveal the weak-

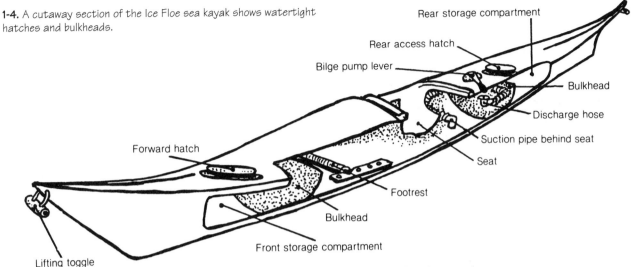

1-4. A cutaway section of the Ice Floe sea kayak shows watertight hatches and bulkheads.

Rear storage compartment

Rear access hatch

Bilge pump lever

Bulkhead

Discharge hose

Suction pipe behind seat

Seat

Forward hatch

Footrest

Bulkhead

Front storage compartment

Lifting toggle

ness in any design. Steve Sinclair, head guide and instructor of the Force 10 Ocean White Water Tours group, is accustomed to taking groups of people out to sea in rough conditions. He had this to say at the end of a training and rescue session I ran in a particularly exposed part of San Francisco Bay: "Most models could barely withstand the rigors of the various rescue procedures. The bottoms and decks cracked under the stress of basic rescue procedures. This demonstrated to me what I have felt for some time: that most ocean kayaks I have seen are much too flimsy for actual ocean kayaking."

North American kayak manufacturers in particular have tended to place more emphasis on lightness than strength and rigidity. Until recently this has been a source of potential problems, but with the introduction of new and more sophisticated materials it is now possible to construct lightweight kayaks without sacrificing the necessary strength. Make sure, however, that any lightweight model you consider purchasing has been thoroughly tested and can stand up under rescue conditions.

Another thing to consider when purchasing a lightweight kayak is that sea kayaks must have sufficient weight to provide momentum when paddling in rough conditions. A kayak being pad-

dled at a brisk speed over wave crests may regularly have as much as 6 or 7 feet of its length hanging in the air. If a strong wind is pressing against the beam of a featherweight kayak, the paddler could lose control. To be seaworthy in high winds and the accompanying sea conditions, an unladen kayak should weigh between fifty and sixty pounds.

Outlet

Footrest

Valve

Rubber extrusion

Pickup pipe

1-5. The Lendal foot pump

It is possible to add weight to keep a light-weight kayak manageable in rough seas and high winds. This added weight must not move around inside the hull. Use long, narrow equipment bags, which are held in place against the bottom of the hull by loops of shock cord. These bags should be secured in position when the kayak is near the water's edge and must be distributed evenly fore and aft.

Plastic Sea Kayaks

Plastic whitewater kayaks have been with us now since the 1970s, and over the last few years plastic sea-touring designs have been available, too.

What do we know of polyethylene as a material for boats from the long experience of the whitewater paddler? The following table compares polyethylene with fiberglass.

	Polyethylene (Linear and Cross-Linked)	Fiberglass
Stiffness	Poor	Fair
Weight	Heavy	Medium
Abrasion Resistance	Poor	Fair
Impact Resistance	Very Good	Fair
Price	Inexpensive	Moderately expensive

I list linear and cross-linked polyethylene together here, as they are much more similar to each other than they are to fiberglass. Cross-linked polyethylenes are somewhat superior to linear, but unlike the latter, they cannot be repaired by welding.

So how do plastic sea kayaks hold up compared with conventional fiberglass boats? Not too well, I'm afraid.

Remember that the development of short whitewater designs in vogue at present was partly triggered by the poor stiffness characteristics of polyethylene. But heavy use of block buoyancy within these kayaks was needed to prevent oil-canning (flexing of the hull) and serious wrap-arounds (jackknifing of the hull) associated with rocky river descents.

Sea-touring kayaks have more volume and are longer than whitewater boats but are not subjected to the heavy bending forces encountered in white water—as long as they are kept out of the surf, that is! Even so, they need to have thick skins, which means extra weight. The metal rods and plastic stiffeners I see within most plastic sea kayaks tell me that there are stiffness problems still awaiting an elegant solution.

One problem that does not affect whitewater kayaks, which are "stripped-down" craft, is the difficulty of effectively adding extra pieces to plastic boats. I am thinking particularly of bulkheads, which can be made watertight so easily in fiberglass boats but have presented insuperable difficulties in plastic. I have yet to see a bulkhead in a plastic boat that did not leak. It may not leak at first perhaps, but I overheard a well-known designer of plastic sea kayaks jokingly say, "I guarantee our bulkheads will leak within a month." On reflection, it didn't seem so funny.

One of the joys of owning a sea kayak is being able to customize one's own craft beyond the mere addition of extra bulkheads and hatches. I am thinking of such features as extra recessed deck-line fittings, anchor points for towlines, knee tubes, and compass wells, as well as other bits and pieces that make any nonkayaking months a time for innovation and experiment. This pleasure is denied to the owners of plastic boats.

Add to this the poor abrasion resistance of polyethylene and its lack of aesthetic appeal and you are left only with its price to commend it. Even this is not so competitive when you examine prices of fully fitted-out boats complete with rudders, skegs, hatches, deck-lines, compass housings, and so on. The cost of fitting this equipment to plastic and fiberglass boats is roughly the same.

I doubt whether an experienced sea paddler would seriously contemplate owning a plastic boat, but the outfitter, watching his novice group hurling his boats against a stone jetty in a short chop, will be offering up a silent prayer of thanks to the scientist who invented polyethylene.

One word of caution: Research moves apace, and more progress is being made with unsupported plastics (including polyethylene) than with reinforced plastics (fiberglass).

While I think it is fair to say that plastic sea kayaks are not yet up to the high standards of design and construction now expected of fiberglass craft, new materials will be discovered and new manufacturing processes will be invented. In fact, these processes are here now, but the costs are prohibitive. As costs inevitably fall, the sea-kayaking world will be able to take advantage of these innovative processes, and the gap between the quality of plastic and fiberglass will narrow.

Rudders

Paddlers often discuss whether kayaks should have rudders, and often the decision depends upon the kayak design. Some kayaks are specifically designed not to need a rudder. For example, the Baidarka Explorer (see fig. 1-6), which I designed, has a ridge or keelson that runs the full length of the boat. This enables the boat to grip the water in much the same way an ice skate locks itself onto the ice.

Rudders can undoubtedly be an advantage for some kayak designs. Track deviation in a double kayak is also probably best corrected by using a rudder. This does away with the necessity of leaning the boat over onto one side, which is much more difficult with two paddlers than one.

Most single paddlers who depend on rudders at the beginning of their careers, however, tend to

put them to one side as their skill level increases. For example, paddlers usually learn quickly that most ocean kayaks can be turned easily in bumpy seas by taking advantage of the waves and using the paddle: the boat is spun around by the paddle as the hull pirouettes around on the top of the waves.

Up to the time of this writing, rudders have been rarely used by experienced British paddlers. It is generally held that they are more of a bother than they are worth. They get fouled up in nets or lines, inhibit seal landings and launchings, and always seem to snap, break, or bend at the worst possible time. With the recent emergence of rudder designs incorporating new materials, however, it appears that rudders will be more accepted.

Baidarka Explorer
(16' 10" x 20½')

1-6. The keel on the Baidarka Explorer enables the boat to grip the water like an ice skate locking itself onto the ice. This design makes a rudder or skeg unnecessary.

Orion
(17' x 24')

1-7. The Orion comes in two cockpit sizes. The small cockpit is shown in this illustration. The drop-down skeg has a sliding control that can be seen on the deck, to the right of the cockpit.

If you do decide to use a rudder, be certain that you choose a good design. There are now many excellent rudder designs on the market. One example was designed by Chuck Sherburne for the Odyssea surf ski. Sherburne is a retired aerospace engineer, and his design exhibits the robust features that could be expected from someone who has been connected to that industry. His system requires very little pressure to turn the rudder, yet the footrest is solid on the heel for hard bracing during the normal paddling stroke. Steve Sinclair of the Force 10 unit has been using this type of rudder on his surf skis in all kinds of weather conditions for several years and has found it durable and effective.

Another excellent rudder mechanism (see fig. 1-8) was designed by Frank Goodman. Goodman based his design on a homemade affair used by Paul Caffyn on his epic circumnavigation of Australia. Known as the C-Trim rudder, the whole unit is fastened to a wedge which in turn is either bonded within the stern of the kayak's hull or to some external molding, customized to suit the shape of any kayak. The rudder and its molding could be held in place by wing nuts. For the owner who doesn't mind the trauma of sawing the stern off a favorite boat, the C-Trim can be fitted to most kayaks by simply trimming off the stern plate to fit the cross section of the boat. The rudder is made from moldings in polycarbonate and ABS, which support a fiberglass blade controlled by a foot pedal. The mechanism is fastened to the wedge-shaped block by two M8 setscrews. The fitting instructions are easy to follow, and the whole affair is available in kit form to fit most boats. I have looked at the design closely and it is one of the few I think will stand up to a good deal of use or abuse.

1-8. The C-Trim rudder (designed by Frank Goodman)

Drop-Down Skegs

Far less trouble, and much more aesthetically pleasing than the rudder, is the drop-down skeg. The name really is self-explanatory. A rigid skeg, or fin, is situated within a few feet of the stern of the kayak. The front end of the skeg is held in place by a pivot pin. This enables the fin to be lowered or raised by a control near the cockpit, preferably placed to one side. When not in use the skeg can be drawn up into a slim box inside the rear watertight compartment.

The principle is simple and is based on the premise that when paddled forward in a sidewind, all kayaks will weathercock (their bows will want to head into the wind). When your kayak is paddled with the skeg fully raised, the kayak will behave normally and swing bow into wind. With the skeg fully lowered, the stern will grip the water and the kayak will then swing downwind.

By fine-tuning the skeg up and down, you will soon find a position that cancels the influence of the wind altogether and enables you to paddle forward without resorting to constant and tiring corrective strokes on the windward side.

When launching, take care to avoid picking up small stones in the skeg box. If you do not, the fin will become jammed in the up position and you will wish that you'd included an old knife blade in your repair kit.

Deck Layout

All those involved in ocean touring seem to have their own pet way of rigging out a deck, but one of the most popular systems is shown in figure 1-9.

Plastic toggles (or homemade wooden toggles) are the most comfortable way to carry a kayak. They are also the safest to use when towing a kayak to shore after the misfortune of capsizing outside the surf line. Loops can twist around and trap fingers during the struggle to reach shore. Always check toggles to make sure that the knots inside are secure and the rope ends are heat sealed—a job often neglected by some manufacturers.

All equipment carried inside a kayak must be kept dry. Access to the storage compartments is gained by means of watertight hatches. At present there are two designs favored by touring kayakers. The lid of Frank Goodman's recently designed hatch is made of strong, flexible plastic. This lid fits snugly onto a rigid rim, which can be either bolted onto the kayak or bonded directly into the deck of the boat during manufacturing. A retaining band of stainless steel, which is located in a recess running around the lid, is tensioned by an over-center finger lock. The Henderson hatch is made of strong, rigid plastic and has a cleverly designed screw top lid that allows the outer rim to turn while the center portion of the lid remains stationary. The threads must be kept free from sand and

grit to ensure smooth movement. Releasing the lid with cold hands can be a problem, but paddlers usually overcome this with a simple homemade wooden bar spanner that rests across the lid and grips the lugs around the edge. No matter what type of hatch is used, the lids are less likely to become lost if they are painted a bright color or fastened to the inside of the hull with a long string. When tightening screw hatches, take care not to start on a cross thread. If any long items of equipment such as a rifle or fishing rod are to be carried, then a third hatch fitted in the forward bulkhead will make storage easy.

The paddle park prevents the paddle from wandering away during filming, rescuing, fishing, or eating. The one I use started life as a broom clip.

Grab lines around the deck should be tight and stay that way. Some like to have grab lines around the reardeck, but I do not think this is necessary. Tensioning is also useful for fastening a kayak to a car's roof rack.

The chart table and compass are held by shock cords. Some paddlers prefer to have their compass more forward and to house it in custom-built deck recesses.

Recessed deck fittings keep the grab lines close to the deck. With no protrusions there is less possibility of damage or injury during deep-water rescues. If your kayak has an inadequate number of deck fittings, figure 1-10 details a method of creating your own.

The small bilge pump can be fitted for either right- or left-hand use. The suction hose can be extra long so that the paddler can help others empty out their boats if necessary.

The towline is a very important item of emergency equipment. It is best to anchor it just behind the cockpit with either a jam cleat or a rope loop fiberglassed into the deck. Use a quick-release knot. The line is then passed through a spliced eye or one made from plastic at the stern and led for-

Toggles

Frank Goodman
hatch

Henderson
hatch

Hatch

Grab lines

Paddle park

Chart table

Recessed
deck fitting

1-9. A popular deck layout for
sea touring

Containers for first aid
and repair kits

Bilge pump

Pump
discharge
outlet

Towline

Hatch

Spare
paddles

Flare
containers

ROCKET FLARE

1-11. *Stuff box for towline*
Make a stuff box using the same method as in figure 1-10. The box shape is made from thin cardboard, which is glued or taped together and then covered with fiberglass matting (A). When the fiberglass has hardened, the cardboard liner can be left to rot away. A slot, which is wide at one end and tapered at the other, should be cut into the deck. The end of the towline is held in position by the knot that slides into the tapered slot (B). A loop of shock cord, which forms part of the towline, provides enough tension to keep the line in place. The box holds the remaining 3 to 4 feet of line.

1-10. *Recessed deck fitting*
Make a small cup by cutting a table-tennis ball in half and reinforcing it with a square of fiberglass mat where the holes will be drilled (A). Trace a circle on the deck where the cup is to be placed and drill two holes inside the circle (B). To hold the cup in place, pass a piece of strong thread through two pinholes pricked in the cup. Lead the thread through the holes in the deck (C). Tightly tie the thread to secure the cup (D). Turn the boat upside down and apply a piece of resin-soaked fiberglass mat over the cup. As soon as the fiberglass hardens, deck line can be passed through the two holes (E). If the fitting is to be used for deck shock cord elastics, make one of the holes large enough for the knot to pass through (F).

ward again to terminate at some convenient point just behind the cockpit. Everyone seems to have a favorite system for towline arrangement. My own system of anchoring the free end of the towline is by means of a stuff box (fig. 1-11), but whichever system is used should be one that can be employed quickly and cause no danger to the person towing, should he accidentally capsize. Although nylon rope will stretch with the strain of towing, a loop of shock cord can be incorporated into the towline, so as to relieve any sudden shocks that may occur when the line is used in rough weather. Shock cord is best joined by a fisherman's knot or by using crimps made from stainless steel. To keep the elastic from snapping and parting the line, the shock cord should be fixed across a loop in the line, so that even if the elastic gives out the rope is still in one piece.

Carry spare paddles on the reardeck, held on by tightly stretched shock cord.

Position the discharge outlet for the pump so

1-12. The author's kayak, as viewed from above, presents a clear picture of the deck line layout. (Photo courtesy Bill Moore)

that the discharged water does not shoot up the arm of the operator.

Flare containers can be made of plumbers' plastic waste pipe. I carry my flares under the same elastics as the spare paddles. Paint the containers fluorescent orange and make a note of the expiration date of the flares.

Containers holding first-aid and repair kits should be stored in the space behind the seat. A sponge should be carried under the seat to help keep the boat clean and dry.

EQUIPMENT

Basic Equipment

Paddles

During those far-off days when my wood and canvas PBK 10 (an early kayak) and I were inseparable, I used to paddle out to sea using a nicely varnished pair of all-wooden paddles joined in the center with a shiny brass ferrule. When one of these paddles stood next to me on the ground, the top of it was almost lost in the clouds. It had to be long because, although the boat I paddled was only slightly over ten feet long, it was thirty-three inches wide, and a paddle any shorter would have meant leaving the best part of my knuckles on the gunwale.

As kayaks became narrower, paddles became shorter. Since sea paddlers had no guideline for determining the best paddle length for these narrow kayaks, they used the river paddler's standard as a guide. By this standard the paddler should be able to reach up and hook her fingers over the top of the blade when the paddle is standing upright in front of her.

To be most effective, a paddle must possess certain qualities. It should be comfortable to hold, and it should be strong. In order to minimize turbulence, the blade must enter the water smoothly, without creating any splash. When a paddle enters the water, any splashing is energy wasted. Curved blades enter the water without disturbing the surface, and an asymmetrical curved blade will do

It is propelled by a two-bladed paddle, which is held in the middle and dipped in the water on each side in turn, like the paddles we use in canoes. It has probably been developed from the Indians' one-bladed paddles. Among the Eskimos on the southwest coast of Alaska the one-bladed paddle is universal; not until we come north of the Yukon River do we find two-bladed paddles, and even there the single blade is still the more common. Further north and eastward along the American coast both forms are found, until the two blades at last come into exclusive use eastward of the Mackenzie River.

The Aleutians seem, strangely enough, to be acquainted with only the two-bladed paddle, and this is also the case, so far as I can gather, with the Asiatic Eskimos. (Nansen, Eskimo Life, *pp. 48–49.)*

this even more smoothly. Once the blade is immersed, any air around the blade—shown by white bubbles—will reduce its efficiency. Air is dragged down as the paddle enters the water. This is more noticeable around the back of the blade. Once in the water, a paddle blade must create drag—it must grip the water. The surface area of the blade is a crucial factor here. The most efficient are called "spoon blades." These are curved widthwise as well as lengthwise. The very curve that gives the propulsion, however, is too great to allow the blade to slice in and out of the sea without splash. Because of this, a compromise has to be reached, and the curves are reduced so that both operations are provided for.

Although curved blades do well at creating little splash, they do have more tendency than paddles with other shapes to flutter. Fluttering is caused by the eddies and vortices that break away from the edge of the blade. Alternately, vortices break away from the edge and cause pressures to build up on the face of the blade. Because the face of the blade cannot make way against the pressures, the paddle will begin to move quickly from side to side—or flutter. Fluttering reduces the efficiency of the stroke and can be disturbing because the paddle feels unsteady in the hand.

Curved blades are more efficient than any other kind of paddle for the high racing stroke. But in a strong beam wind, a long, thin paddle is less likely to be caught by severe gusts. This is because the long, thin paddle can be completely immersed in the water at a more acute angle and the upper blade is consequently lower during the stroke. For this reason, the long, thin blade is the type of paddle I prefer. My paddling colleagues are divided in their preferences between the long, thin paddle (such as the Seamaster) and the asymmetric curved paddle (such as the Nordcapp).

Paddle weight is as important as paddle length. Paddles should be light as well as strong in order to withstand many hours of use. I like a pad-

dle that has sufficient weight to maintain momentum during the forward stroke. I also favor a shaft that flexes slightly. To make paddling more comfortable and to give a more positive grip on the shaft during an Eskimo roll, the shaft should have a slightly oval shape where the hands grip and are at right angles to the nearest blade.

Paddle Leash

The paddle leash (fig. 2-1) is an indispensable means of keeping paddle and paddler together. A paddle leash of thin shock cord is simple to make, and it can be worth its weight in gold. No matter what the circumstances or how rough the sea, the paddle will never become parted from the paddler. To join the elastic, simply crimp it together with precut pieces of stainless steel or bind it with twine.

Clothing

Kayaking on the sea is a dry sport—or so I keep trying to tell everybody. Novices do get wet, however. On their bottom half, beginners should wear high-waisted wet-suit trousers made of three to four millimeter neoprene or long johns that have shoulder straps. On their top half, they should

2-1. *The paddle leash*

wear any warm, comfortable clothing. Polypropylene is very popular, but whatever is chosen must be kept dry by a waterproof anorak. Some years ago, I designed one based on an Inuit hunter's kayak smock, and it has proved very popular.

Full wet-suit jackets can cause chafing and fatigue. Novices who insist on wearing one should make sure there is plenty of room around the armpits or cut the arms out altogether.

Feet should be protected from the cold and wet, but the footwear chosen should also be solid enough to allow the kayaker to walk comfortably over stones or slippery rocks during landings. Most experienced paddlers wear knee-high rubber boots with warm socks. They have also discarded neoprene trousers for something more comfortable. I wear track suit bottoms made of double force material and covered by high-waisted waterproof sailing trousers. Dry suits specially designed for kayakers are becoming popular in colder climates.

The decision to cast off sweaty neoprene gear for the comfort of fiberpile and waterproofs is a serious one that should be made only by experienced paddlers. If there is the remotest chance of being immersed in cold water, stay with the neoprene.

Pogies

Cold hands can make paddling uncomfortable, and in cold weather the experience can be almost unbearable. Gloves are not completely satisfactory because they tend to destroy the feel for the paddle shaft. There are a number of solutions. Neoprene Smittens (fig. 2-2) can be used. These are made by Valley Canoe Products in Britain. The simpler muffins (fig. 2-3) are equally satisfactory. Both of these items fall into the general category of "pogies."

Headgear

Headgear is important, and what you wear depends very much on what you are going to do

2-2. Neoprene Smittens designed by Frank Goodman

2-3. Muffins protect the hands from cold winds without constricting the wrist.

and where you intend to do it. Most paddlers wear crash helmets for surfing, but in cold weather these can also be worn over a neoprene hat for extra warmth. It is sometimes advisable to wear a crash helmet for deep-water rescue practices, especially when these are conducted in rough conditions. For normal paddling in cold weather, a wool hat can provide the necessary protection or the hood of an anorak can be worn over a large peaked truckers' hat. The large peak gives excellent facial protection when paddling head into

In fair weather the kaiak-man uses the so-called half-jacket (akuilisak). This is made of water-tight skin with the hair removed, and is sewn with sinews. Round its lower margin runs a drawstring, or rather a draw thong, by means of which the edge of the jacket can be made to fit so closely to the kaiak-ring that it can only be pressed and drawn down over it with some little trouble. This done, the half-jacket forms, as it were, a watertight extension of the kaiak. The upper margin of the jacket comes close up to the armpits of the kaiak-man. . . .

Loose sleeves of skin are drawn over the arms, and are lashed to the overarm and to the wrist, thus preventing the arm from becoming wet. Watertight mittens of skin are drawn over the hands. This half-jacket is enough to keep out the smaller waves which wash over the kaiak. In a heavier sea, on the other hand, the whole-jacket (tuilik) is used. This is made in the same way as the half-jacket, and, like it, fits close to the kaiak-ring, but is longer above, has sleeves attached to it, and a hood which comes right over the head. It is laced tight round the face and wrists, so that with it on the kaiak-man can go right through the breakers and can capsize and right himself again, without getting wet and without letting a drop of water into the kaiak. (Nansen, Eskimo Life, pp. 49–51.)

wind and is very similar in its protection qualities to the peaked headgear worn by the old-time Aleuts when they were engaged in sea otter hunting. Too much sun can be dangerous, and the reflection off the water can even burn the lips. Choose a hat therefore that gives protection all around from the hot sun. If the warmth of the sun causes overheating, it is time well spent to stop and remove a few layers of clothing.

Poncho

A poncho keeps off the rain and, at the same time, allows air to circulate and prevents condensation. One that can double as a bivouac tent is useful in survival situations and also makes changing out of wet clothes in the open a bearable experience. Choose one that is a bright fluorescent color to double as a rescue marker.

Personal Flotation Devices

The only suitable personal flotation device (PFD) is the life jacket which, unlike the buoyancy aid, is designed to float the head of an unconscious person above water. All beginners should wear a life jacket at *all* times. Because of the awkward and ungainly shape of some PFDs that have integral buoyancy already included inside, most experienced paddlers wear buoyancy aids that do not have any self-righting facility. On long trips in calm seas and in the company of others, the experienced paddler may not wear a buoyancy aid, but carries it within easy reach under deck elastics to be worn for difficult landings or when weather conditions are bad. A cautionary word about life jackets: If they are worn with trousers made of neoprene, the buoyancy effect of the trousers will cause legs and feet to rise to the surface and thus cancel the self-righting quality of the life jacket.

In the United States, the law governing use of PFDs differs from state to state. In some areas the life jacket need only be carried, while in others it must be worn. In the United Kingdom, wearing a life jacket is only recommended.

Waterproof Bags and Containers

Any equipment stowed inside a kayak *must stay dry*—survival could depend on it. The salt water that seeps into worn, badly tied, or poorly repaired waterproof bags and ruins clothing, food supplies, sleeping bags, and cameras could be fatal to anyone involved in an extended sea trip. It also could be an intolerable burden on the rest of the party. In a situation where individuals carry items of a special nature, to be used by the rest of the group (medical supplies, cameras and film, radio equipment, and, in some instances, firearms and ammunition), any loss or damage could blunt the efficiency of the group and may put them in grave danger.

Any bag or container can be used as long as it can be opened and closed repeatedly without damage. Good serviceable bags can be made from ex-Army capes and groundsheets. Plastic trash bags are hardly suitable. I prefer to use bags that are specially designed to fit through the deck hatch openings. Naturally, if your kayak has one of the smaller hatches, you must be prepared to transfer items such as sleeping bags and tents into these new narrow bags. With these bags packing for a long trip may take a little more time, but care and consideration are a small price to pay for dry gear.

Equipment carried inside watertight compartments also should be protected inside waterproof bags, just in case a rock or other object puts a hole in the kayak.

All bags and containers should be made secure so that in the event of a capsize they stay with the boat and do not entangle the paddler in long, untidy securing lines.

First-Aid and Emergency Kits

An emergency-repair kit (fig. 2-4) and a small

Swiss Army knife	Epoxy glue
Copper wire	Sharpening stone
Pliers	Plastic bag containing toilet
Precut stainless steel clips (for joining shock cord elastic)	paper and coins
	Waterproof torch
	Firelighting tablets
Cord (for spare bow loop)	Signaling mirror
Patches or duct tape	Fishing line
Adhesive	Fishhooks and weight
Scissors	Small can opener
Sail needle	Coil of thin, strong line
Terylene thread	Heavy-duty polyethylene
Sailors palm	exposure bag
Waterproof matches	Patch kit (resin, catalyst,
Candle stump	and fiberglass mat)
Bottle of acetone	

2-4. *These are essential items for an emergency-repair kit.*

Assorted bandaids	Antibacterial ointment
Assorted bandages (ace, triangular, etc.)	Antihistamine cream
	Sun protection
Adhesive tape	Snake-bite serum
Gauze roll	Scissors
Water purification tablets	Tweezers
Aspirin	Safety pins
Seasickness pills	Plastic tubing and an airway
Pain killer	(such as a Brooks airway)
Antiseptic cream	First-aid book

2-5. *These items should be included in a small first-aid kit.*

first-aid kit (fig. 2-5) should be carried permanently inside the kayak. These items should be adequate for day trips and short jaunts.

Figure 2-6 lists the contents of a first-aid kit for an extended trip. The items listed should suffice for four to six people for a two-month trip. Also include any specialized items that would normally be carried in the small kit, such as the Brooks airway (fig. 2-7). For some areas it may be necessary to include snake-bite serum. Complete the first-aid kit with a copy of an up-to-date first-aid book.

For British travelers, the normally generous National Health Service does not supply medication for trips abroad (other than for a preexisting

Basic Kit for 4 or 5 People

Dressings
  Adhesive bandages (50 assorted sizes)
  Elastic bandages (two, 3" x 5')
  Butterfly bandages (assorted sizes)
  Gauze rolls (one, 2" and one, 3")
  Triangular bandage (one, 40")
  Gauze squares (twelve, 3" x 3" and twelve, 4" x 4")
  Compresses (assorted)
  Adhesive tape (two rolls, one, 2" and one, 3")
  Cotton wool pack (compressed)

Cleansing
  Bar sop or mild disinfectant

Instruments
  Scissors (2 pair, blunt and sharp)
  Forceps (1 pair)
  Sterile scalpel blade (1)
  Safety pins (4)
  Thermometers (2)
  Disposable syringes and needles
  Suture material
  Paper and ballpoint pen (to note drugs given)

Medicines
  Aspirin or acetaminophen (100 tablets)
  Painkillers*
  Antibiotics*
  Sedatives*
  Antihistamines*
  Diarrhea medications*
  Laxatives*
  Coated sodium (20 tablets)
  Antiworm medication*

Anti-inflammatory eye- and eardrops*
Oil of cloves for toothache
Temporary tooth filling material**

Topical medications
  Sunscreen (2 tubes)
  Zinc oxide ointment or Vaseline
  Lip balm with sunscreen (1 tube)
  Calamine cream (1 tube)
  Insect repellent
  Lotrimin ointment for fungal infections (1 tube)
  Mercurochrome or tincture of iodine
  Louse or insect powder
  Anusol for hemorrhoids (10 suppositories)
  Antimalarial medication***
  Rubbing alcohol

Individual Kit
Dressings
  Adhesive bandages (assorted sizes)
  Gauze bandages (3" x 3")

Instruments
  Razor blade
  Paper and ballpoint pen (to note drugs given)

Medicines
  Aspirin or acetaminophen (100 tablets)
  Antibiotics*
  Personal prescriptions*
  Diarrhea medications*
  Anti-inflammatory eye- and eardrops*
  Iodine-based water purifying tablets (100)

Topical medications
  Sunscreen (1 tube)
  Zinc oxide ointment or Vaseline

  * Consult a physician for specific prescriptions.
 ** Consult a dentist to obtain.
*** Consult a physician for medication appropriate to the area you are traveling through.

2-6. This is a basic first-aid kit for an extended trip.

2-7. The Brooks airway

medical condition), and all drugs needed for this purpose have to be purchased—usually at a considerably greater expense than anticipated. Friendly doctors, usually general practitioners, may defray this expense by donating drug samples. Travelers should otherwise ask their doctor to sign the entire list as a private prescription. American travelers should also obtain necessary drugs.

Be sure to take along the prescriptions for the drugs or photocopies of their descriptions (with indication, recommended dosage). In the United States all drugs are listed in *The Physician's Desk Reference,* published annually.

Store the kit in waterproof containers and transfer liquids and tablets into plastic bottles (except for one glass bottle for sting suction) and attach labels with tape because stick-on labels can come off in wet heat. The kit should be accessible at all times and at least one person should be thoroughly familiar with its contents, knowing the exact location of each item.

Climbing Rope

A climbing rope is useful for lowering kayaks and equipment down cliffs and essential for rescue purposes in the event of glacier walking. Although the rope will be heavy and bulky, it can be carried slung under the deck between a paddler's legs. Wrap the rope in a polyethylene bag to keep it in good condition.

Fog Horn

Do not bother with the gas-operated fog horn—it never seems to work when most needed. The best and most reliable fog horn is lung-operated. Little can go wrong with it and the blast is quite ear-shattering. Make sure the fog horn is fastened to the kayak by a long cord.

Fog horns are used for the following:

- To signal groups on land.
- To control groups on the water.
- To frighten bears.
- To make a distress call.
- To avoid being run down in busy shipping lanes under foggy conditions. Sounding the signal "D"—*one long blast and two short blasts*—will let vessels know that you maneuver with difficulty, and they should keep clear.

Special Equipment

The Pod

For those who nurture the uncontrollable urge to paddle alone on the sea, an item of equipment worth considering is the pod (fig. 2-8).

The pod is a fiberglass capsule, designed by Alan Byde, that seals off the space needed by the paddler from the rest of the kayak's hull. In the event of a capsize, the water that enters the pod can be measured in pints rather than gallons. In fact, the pod limits the amount of water that enters the boat to such an extent that emptying the kayak and the rescues I describe in later chapters are totally unnecessary.

Like most good ideas, the pod was developed by trial and error. Byde was originally influenced by the Chaussette, or kneeling bag, as used by C-1 and C-2 (one-man Canadian and two-man Canadian) white-water paddlers. This canvas bag was secured to the manhole rim and gave the paddler

2-8. The pod

2-9. The cockpit liner

a separate compartment sealed off from the main body of the hull. If the occupant was forced to leave the boat during a capsize, only the bag filled with water, and this was easily emptied by turning the bag inside out.

Applying this principle to a seagoing kayak, Byde first of all designed a fiberglass cockpit liner (fig. 2-9). It was made in two halves for easy fitting and consisted of a foot box and a bucket seat. The foot box was fitted into the kayak first and fiberglassed against the underside of the deck. The seat was fitted next by joining that molding to the foot box and then fiberglassing the upper rim of the seat molding around the underside of the cockpit. This liner could be installed in almost any fiberglass kayak and fit almost any size paddler (at least up to 34 inches of inside leg and size twelve shoe). Although the liner was easy to fit, a cockpit rim appropriate to the kayak was still required as a separate item. The additional weight of the liner, however, was negligible, and a kayak fitted with a liner weighed approximately only half a kilo more than a boat fitted with a conventional seat, bulkheads, and footrest.

Unfortunately, for a number of reasons, the liner proved impractical to market. The whole idea had to be rethought, and eventually the one-piece pod capsule was born. This self-contained unit has thigh braces to permit rolling, and the rim of the pod is attached to a mating rim on the kayak, which is formed inside the deck opening.

A pod or cockpit liner makes it possible to roll a kayak without the use of a spray cover. This is ideal if a reentry and roll have to be performed, as it makes emptying out afterward completely unnecessary.

The pod is shaped so that the cockpit almost empties itself completely when the kayak is leaned over on its side in the water. The stern of the boat also can be depressed so that the kayak tilts to an angle of about 45 degrees, and the water drains out from the back of the cockpit.

After emptying, there may be a small amount of water left in the pod, but this does not affect the handling of the kayak. As the pod never takes on more than six gallons of water—unless you cheat and fill it with a bucket—even the weakest person or a very young child can maneuver the kayak into an emptying position.

The pod also reinforces the center section of the kayak. If the paddler has the misfortune of wrapping his kayak around a jetty support, fish trap, or tree, and the current is strong, the boat will not fold up around the paddler's legs amidships, thereby trapping him; it will shear off behind the cockpit.

Obviously a pod will not prevent a kayak from being wrecked, but it will allow the paddler to escape from the wreck.

Whether the pod becomes a popular addition to commercially built kayaks remains to be seen.

At present, this undoubtedly safe accessory is available only if kayak owners are prepared to have one fitted as a separate item after they have purchased their boat. Looking back over the years, however, I can recall numerous instances where a great deal of sweat, heartache, and nervous tension could have been saved if my companions had possessed podded kayaks.

In 1988 a near tragedy on the Irish Sea highlighted a hitherto unforeseen problem. On a rough sea, a paddler became aware that a hole in the hull of his boat was causing it to take in large quantities of water. Before long his kayak, which was fitted with a pod, became unmanageable. Luckily for the paddler, his distress did not go unnoticed, and he was eventually winched to safety by a helicopter.

It became obvious that an accidental hole anywhere in the hull of a kayak so equipped would allow water to gain unrestricted entry into the main body of the sealed interior. Without the constraints of bulkheads, and in any kind of swell, this uncontrolled water would swill from end to end, severely influencing the kayak's handling capabilities.

If water pours into a boat fitted with the usual bulkheads, the pressure builds until eventually no more water can get in. The air thus trapped, together with the buoyancy provided by the undamaged compartments, helps to keep the kayak and its occupant on the surface and mobile. If, however, the kayak has even the slightest leak above the waterline, the air will escape and the pressure will be lost, allowing more water to enter. Nevertheless, there will still be enough overall buoyancy in the kayak to support the paddler.

A leak above the waterline in a podded boat will, in like manner, cause air to escape, pressure to be lost, and more water to enter. Unfortunately, without bulkheads, the consequence may well be a fully swamped kayak. Even where a leak is small and air pressure loss is minimal, the water that enters will naturally slop from end to end of the hull with no bulkheads to limit or restrain it. Even if the kayak is not completely swamped, it will be extremely difficult to control in rough conditions.

The only practical way to get rid of the water inside a kayak fitted with a sealed cockpit liner is to remove the hatches prior to a deep-water rescue. The practice of removing hatches on the open sea has always been deplored for safety reasons. Even hatches secured by string and light chains have been torn away in the heat of rough-water rescues. For this reason, I design all my kayaks so that an unaccompanied paddler would find it almost impossible to remove his own hatches.

Of course, one has to be realistic and recognize that leaks are not restricted to podded boats. It may be necessary to empty water from the compartment of a kayak fitted with bulkheads. In this case, however, the open hatch does not lead into the main body of the kayak's hull, and even if the rescue goes badly, the horror of a complete swamping is not a constant threat.

Most leading kayak designers agree that the only way to make pods completely safe is to fit them with bulkheads. Until a better system emerges, I definitely support this conclusion.

Drogue

I can think of a number of situations when a paddler's discomfort might be eased if the bow of a kayak—whether for one paddler or two—can be maintained head to wind without any effort on the part of the paddler. You may want either to keep dry and sit out a storm without undue drifting or to ensure the stability of the kayak while fishing, eating, relieving yourself, flying your kite for pleasure not propulsion, or even snuggling down inside the hull to sleep. Whatever the reason, a strong, well-designed drogue (or sea anchor; see fig. 2-10) will create enough drag in the water to swing the bow or the stern into the weather—depending on where the drogue is anchored. For instance, if you are flying a kite, it might be prudent to drogue from the stern.

Once you have fitted your drogue, it would be wise to test it inside the surf line—a small surf will do fine. After all, how often do you get two-foot breaking seas on the open ocean?

Figure 2-10 shows a reliable design, which is less bothersome to handle than the multi-string parachute type. The drogue is made of a canvas-

2-10. *The drogue*

type material and is open at both ends. The line, of an overall length of approximately thirty feet, passes through the bow loop. The drogue line is fastened to the deck line, and the end of the trip line is secured within easy reach.

Radar Reflector

It is not wise to play in busy shipping lanes. The danger of being run down in dense fog is great, especially by ships that travel fast or have difficulty in maneuvering. A radar reflector is a device used by boats of all sizes to reflect the radar waves given off vessels that carry radar equipment as part of their navigational aids. If the reflector is hung in a prominent position, it should enable shipping or rescue services to be aware of a paddler's presence in busy shipping areas.

If you want to make a long-lasting radar reflector that has a professional look, proceed as follows (see fig. 2-11).

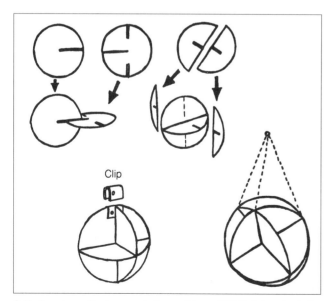

2-11. A radar reflector, made from sixteen S.W.G. (standard wire gauge) aluminum or aluminum alloy, will enable ships to detect the presence of a kayaker in a busy shipping lane.

Make the reflector from aluminum and be sure all the faces are at *right angles to each other at all times*. The higher the reflector is placed above sea level the better. Paint it fluorescent orange to increase visibility. Make it not less than 8 inches in diameter. Suspend it by a strong cord in the "rain catching position," or so the apex of the three uppermost segments points downward, as illustrated. Remember that even a good reflector can be rendered useless when hung up incorrectly.

Reflectors made of aluminum can be a little cumbersome, however. An alternative is to lightly form some kitchen foil into a ball about 9 inches in diameter and pack it in an open-mesh bag. Either hang this up on the end of a thin rod to increase the range or stick it under the reardeck elastics. I did some tests with the Northumbria River Police boat and discovered that with the foil I gave off a blip equal to that emitted by quite a large fishing boat or a navigation buoy. This can keep morale high when it is foggy and there is a lot of traffic about.

Bang Stick

There are parts of the world where an attack by sharks could be high on the list of hazards faced by the kayak paddler. In such an area, carrying a device known as a bang stick (fig. 2-12) is a useful precaution. (Also see discussion under Sharks in chapter on hazardous wildlife.)

A 12- or 20-gauge shotgun cartridge is contained in a special holder at the end of a long steel rod. A split pin holds the firing pin clear of the cartridge. The power head is made to fit over the point of a normal fish spear without threading.

To operate the bang stick, first remove the safety clip. Once this is done, the explosive charge is fired by pushing the power head against a firm surface. The effect is twofold: The prey is injured and it is also affected by the shockwave of the explosion.

2-12. The bang stick

There are two precautions worth taking: Secure the safety clip so that it cannot become lost, and do not hold the bang stick in line with any part of your body. Unless the bang stick is completely submerged, the recoil will not be absorbed by the water.

Firearms

There are three reasons why it may be necessary to carry some kind of firearm with normal kayaking equipment: to kill to eat, to prevent something from eating you, or to protect yourself from other humans (fortunately, this applies only to some parts of the world). These conditions usually will occur during expeditions to wilderness areas.

Killing to eat means filling a cooking pot and not, please note, filling a freezer. Because of this I give no instructions on how to kill a caribou.

To kill small animals and birds the best choice will be a good quality bolt action .22-caliber rifle. Bolt action weapons are traditionally reliable, accurate, and easy to repair and maintain. I do not recommend shooting small fry with .440-caliber Magnum repeating rifles, as there will be very little left to eat.

Animals that might eat you are usually also very large, and will move very quickly. Taking into

consideration that you are probably not the world's best shot—especially when your hand is shaking with understandable anxiety—and that the animal has to be stopped at all costs, I would recommend the 12-gauge short-barreled shotgun loaded with a solid slug. It is a pump action weapon and can be fitted with a pistol grip and a folding stock. Because of its size when folded, it is ideal to store inside a kayak. Keep it in a waterproof bag and sling it underneath the foredeck between your knees.

During normal camp activities, the gun should be left in a place known to everyone, and it should be left in the same firing condition each time. You might keep it *loaded* with the *safety catch off,* but *without a round in the breech*. If it has to be fired in a hurry—one pump—then bang; there is no time wasted wondering if the safety catch is on or off or whether or not the gun needs cocking.

A few years ago a picture appeared on the front cover of *Canoeing* magazine showing Dr. Mike Jones crouching down next to his kayak loading a revolver. The photo was taken during an expedition he led down the Blue Nile, and the weapon was used for protection against crocodiles and bandits. These bandits actually fired on him during the expedition and it brought home to me the fact that there are still remote parts of the world where travelers can be killed for no other reason than the food and medical supplies they carry. If research indicates that problems of this nature are likely to occur, seek advice from the appropriate government department in the country you intend to visit. Inquiries regarding the suitability of various types of weapons are best directed to local police or army units. If approached correctly, I have found both to be sympathetic and informative on the subject of firearms. Information from travelers who have already passed through the area you intend to visit also is invaluable. News in wilderness areas travels fast, and it will soon become known that you have taken precautions to defend yourself and that you would not be easy pickings for those who might have designs on your equipment.

You cannot be too careful with loaded firearms. Leaders of expeditions should make sure that members of the group have had proper weapon training, otherwise someone is going to have a foot blown off—or worse!

Revolvers should always be carried with one chamber empty, and that chamber should be the one next to the firing pin.

Rifles should never be cocked—i.e., a cartridge should not be fed into the breech—unless the gun is to be fired immediately.

Salt water and sweaty hands will ruin any firearm, so check, oil, and clean firearms daily.

Most ammunition is waterproof, and that includes shotgun cartridges, but any rounds that are stored in wet bags inside a kayak will start to corrode. Although this will not stop the round from being fired, it will probably stop it from being ejected because the empty cartridge will stick in the breech and thus render the gun useless after the first shot.

KAYAK STROKES AND MANEUVERS

Proficiency

Unlike folding boats, modern sea kayaks do not breed "instant" kayakers, and paddlers should master the techniques necessary to become proficient ocean kayakers.* Let me define exactly what I consider to be a proficient sea kayaker.

As far as practical skills are concerned, the proficient paddler should be able to:

- Paddle 15–20 miles in a day's trip.
- Paddle a kayak out through at least 4-foot breakers and into open water, then back in again, then forward and backward without capsizing.
- Tow the kayak ashore in the event of a capsize, and maintain contact not only with the kayak, but with the paddle and equipment.
- Turn a kayak around through 360 degrees using forward and reverse sweep strokes. This should be done as quickly as the design of the boat will allow.
- Move a kayak sideways by means of a draw stroke or a sculling draw stroke.

* The British Canoe Union tests for Sea Proficiency, Advanced Proficiency, and Senior Instructor's Award are to be found in Appendix 1.

- Prevent a kayak from capsizing using a sculling for support stroke and also a slap support stroke.
- Steer a kayak with a stern rudder while traveling down the face of a small wave, then allow the kayak to come broadside on to a breaking wave and then, with a high brace, keep the boat upright as the wave breaks over it.
- Assist another kayaker in emptying out the kayak of a third person who has capsized and then put the person back in the boat.

All of the aforementioned strokes and maneuvers should be possible at this stage in moderate

> The youthful rivals must also exercise their ability among sunken cliffs and dashing surges, now driven between a double wave upon the rocks, now whirled completely round, or buried in the foam. In this rough school, initiated into these perilous gymnastics, they learn to bid defiance to the heaviest tempest, and to conduct their barks to land through the rage of contending elements. (Crantz, History of Greenland, p. 141.)

The Eskimo "Kayaks" were, of course, a great attraction to us strangers, and as soon as possible I possessed myself of one. The necessary balance in this narrow, crank little vessel is very difficult for a beginner to acquire. One feels as if he were swinging on a knife-edge, and it is very necessary, so to speak, to keep your hair parted well in the middle. Yet when one sees the Eskimo dancing like seabirds on the crests of the waves the whole performance seems simply child's play. As soon as my "Kayak" was ready I took it down to the shore. I found it no easy matter to force my legs and as much else of me as was necessary through the narrow opening into the place where I was to sit. This done, I was carefully pushed out into the water, but the feeling that seized me just as I left dry land was one of unspeakable insecurity. The little craft rocked first to one side then the other, and every moment promised an immediate capsize. It seemed to me a simple impossibility that I should ever learn to sit it, and I looked with despairing envy and desire at the Eskimo, who were of course out to enjoy the sight of Nalagak in a "Kayak," and were darting hither and thither over the water, and throwing their little spears about with as much ease and indifference as if they were sitting safe on the floor at home. But practice has a wonderful effect, and after one or two outings I began to feel tolerably comfortable. I got on better still when I had a pair of outriggers or supports made to help me. These are miniature "Kayaks," about two feet long, and are fastened on each side of the canoe, just behind the seat. They make things considerably easier for the uninitiated of course, but the Eskimo themselves rarely use them, and I myself abandoned them after a while.

(Fridtjof Nansen, The First Crossing of Greenland, *trans. Hubert Majendie Gepp [London: Longmans, Green, and Co., 1892], pp. 402–3.)*

weather conditions—winds of Force 4 and a swell of five feet. I have not mentioned the Eskimo roll, as I consider that any proficient kayaker should not have to resort to this advanced maneuver in moderate weather conditions.

All proficient sea kayakers should have a sound knowledge of elementary seamanship, including:

- The effect of tides and how to allow for them and the influence they have on the surface of the sea, having special regard to overfalls, rips, and races.
- Elementary meteorology and its effect on paddling conditions.
- Coastal and offshore navigation. The aspiring kayaker should be able to plan sea journeys using a nautical chart, tide tables, a *Tidal Stream Atlas,* a volume of the *Coastal Pilot* for the area, and if necessary a topographical map to plan suitable campsites.

At all times the proficient sea kayaker will carry spare paddles, flares, torch, compass, whistle or fog horn, a change of clothing, some emergency food (chocolate or candy bars), the means of making a hot drink, a first-aid kit (including a polyethylene exposure bag), and a repair kit for the kayak and accessories.

All equipment should be serviceable and well maintained. All bags and containers must be completely watertight. In some parts of the world certain items of equipment will be dictated by local circumstances. Some examples would be firearms for protection against wild animals or local bandits, a bang stick for sharks, or a mosquito head net for the smaller varieties of wild beast.

With the necessary free time, a little determination, the correct equipment, good conditions in which to practice, and someone to offer guidance at the appropriate times, an individual can become proficient in handling a sea kayak in a couple of months or even weeks. Of course, complete competence is achieved only through experience. Unlike the case with novices in many other physical sports, it is rare for any enthusiastic novice sea kayaker to feel handicapped by mere years. Nor is it necessary for those over thirty, forty, fifty, or even sixty years old to fade away from top level sea kayaking. It would appear that, with our sport, what one loses in youth and speed is often vastly outweighed by maturity, experience, and sheer exuberance.

Maneuvers

Beach Launch

For the basic and simple beach launch (fig. 3-1A) place the kayak on the sand at the waterline and seat yourself with the paddle held upright in one hand. Then use your free hand to push the boat toward the water and at the same time hitch forward with your body until the kayak is afloat.

If there is any surf running, time your launch so it is made during a lull in the wave patterns. Large swells arrive near the coast in groups or sets

3-1. Basic launching methods include the beach launch (A), the rock launch (B), and the seal launch (C).

3-2. The author goes out through surf at South Shields Beach. He says: "I always seem to get water up my nose when I do this!" (Photo courtesy Jim Appleby)

of six to eight parallel waves. After a set, there is usually a lull of several minutes when the waves diminish considerably. Once on the water, paddle quickly to clear the breaking surf. If a wave appears, take it head on and paddle straight through. Do not lift your arms above your head, but rather lean forward into the wave and keep your head down.

If the beach slopes steeply and there is a dumping surf (i.e., the waves crash down steeply without any run to the beach), it may be necessary to have someone hold your kayak steady at the water's edge and give you a shove during a lull in the waves. In these circumstances the last person off the beach should be the most experienced because there will be nobody to steady his kayak and push him off.

For all beach launchings in very cold conditions, it is advisable to use a small piece of driftwood to push yourself into the water. This will in most cases prevent the discomfort of beginning your paddle with a cold, wet hand.

Rock Launch

For the rock launch (fig. 3-1B) lay your paddle across the rear of the cockpit to form a bridge between the kayak and a rock. Carefully balance with the paddle and sit down by placing your legs one at a time inside the boat. Be sure to lean slightly toward the rock to prevent a capsize seaward. When you are seated and have the spray cover in place, it may be necessary to take the weight off the kayak with the paddle and your free hand so that the kayak can float clear of any rocks that lie just below the surface.

Seal Launch

Launching can be difficult in areas where rocks and cliffs are abundant with no flat beaches to be found, but with careful positioning and timing you can successfully launch in fairly rugged terrain. Figure 3-1C illustrates a seal launch down a rock covered with seaweed. For this launch you position the kayak at the top of the rock or at any place on it where you can balance the kayak for entry. Once seated, hold the paddle upright with one hand and push with the free hand to gain momentum. You must balance carefully as the boat slides down into the water.

Another kind of seal launch (not illustrated) can be attempted if there is a swell running and there are flat rocks available above the level of the water. Position your kayak and seat yourself in it at a point where the larger waves wash up over the higher rock slabs. It should be only a matter of minutes before a swell larger than the rest rises up to lift the kayak off the rock. With careful timing, you can help the water under the hull to float the kayak off the rock: holding your paddle in one hand, partially support the weight of the kayak on your paddle and free hand and at the same time hitch forward with your body.

Side Drop

The side drop launch (fig. 3-3) from the side of a jetty or a similar platform may be used when all other methods prove impossible. It is a difficult maneuver and is best suited for the advanced kayaker, but it is well worth knowing. The side drop can be used when the kayak is 4 to 5 feet above water level. With care it works just as well from greater heights as long as the launching platform and the landing place are clear of obstructions and the water is deep. The side drop can even be used if you have to launch from the side of a small boat. I have never tried this, however, with a fully loaded kayak.

This maneuver is best practiced in a swimming pool, first from the side, then from a low springboard. The boat must be positioned with extreme care so it half rests on the platform and half hangs in space. As you enter the cockpit and prepare for the launch, all your weight must be kept toward the platform or the boat will overturn. Once seated, place the spray cover into position and give the kayak momentum by swinging the paddle forcefully across your body and slightly upward. At the same time jerk your body—with the kayak—

upward and outward into space. During this take-off it is important not to lean too far out because this could cause the kayak to hit the water on its side, and this in turn could cause a capsize. In any event, be prepared to execute a support stroke (high brace) as the kayak hits the water.

Basic Landing

Try to choose an area where the surf is small—at the sides of a bay rather than in the center of it or on a weather shore (a shore lying to the windward). If a surf is running, determine how close you can get to the shore and still remain outside the area where the largest waves are breaking. As with a launch, time your landing so it is made during a lull in wave patterns. Sit and observe the relation between the waves and the lulls. Choose a lull and paddle in on the back of one of the waves (fig. 3-4) as it rolls in toward the

3-3. The side drop is an emergency maneuver performed from a platform or jetty 4 to 5 feet above the water level.

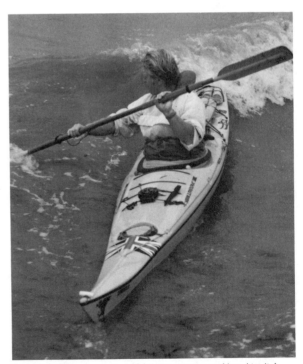

3-4. Landing in a small surf (Photo courtesy Alan Ainslie)

beach. When you paddle on the back of a wave, you work directly against the water particles, which are traveling in the opposite direction (see fig. 3-13, p. 43). As a consequence, your forward progress is retarded, and you will be left behind to wallow in the trough of the wave. This, of course, will put you on the face of the next incoming wave. The danger now is that the boat will surge forward on the face of this new wave. To prevent this and to hold yourself back until the swell has passed, execute a few reverse paddle strokes. As the wave passes beneath you, paddle hard again on its back. You will begin to make headway toward the beach. It may be necessary to repeat this maneuver several times before the waves are small enough to be disregarded and the kayak is in shallow water.

In a group situation, the leader or another experienced paddler appointed by the leader chooses the path to shore and lands ahead of the main party. Once on the beach, this person can view the lines of surf as they approach, time the lulls, and then, using hand signals, direct each paddler into shore. The person on shore can be of particular help to novices who are often reluctant to turn their heads around in surf for fear of losing their balance.

Landing in a Dumping Surf

It is difficult and often dangerous to land in a dumping surf. These waves are caused by a bottom with a steep shelf. Each wave quickly reaches its critical depth and then peaks and breaks suddenly, dragging with it sand and small stones, which rise up inside the curl. The wave and stones crash down on the paddler with great impact. The breaking of a dumping wave is almost as explosive because the air that is trapped and compressed inside the curl exerts tremendous pressure.

In a dumping surf, you still must attempt to take advantage of the lulls between sets of waves. The waves in these lulls are smaller than the waves in the sets. They are, however, still dumping waves. Because of the characteristics of these waves, you must paddle frantically in order to maintain your position on the back of the wave. Even when you are touching ground, you will need to use your paddle and hand to grab into the sand to prevent being sucked back into the next wave.

Again, it is essential that an experienced paddler land first. Not only must he guide and reassure other paddlers as they come in, but he must grab their boats, drag them up into the sand, and hold them steady while they make a hasty exit.

In any kind of surf, it is advisable for inexperienced paddlers to land one at a time and to keep a good distance from one another. It is not necessary for everyone to dash for the same wave or even the same lull.

Seal Landing

The necessity of performing a seal landing (see fig. 3-5) depends on the prevailing conditions. If a landing is necessary and there is no convenient flat beach at hand, it becomes obvious that other plans have to be made. You must improvise and use whatever physical features are at hand. The type of rock you choose to land upon will depend upon the type of local rock formations, but flat rocks will of course give a much softer landing than the more jagged variety.

First select a potential landing spot over which the swell surges from time to time, and where a landing might be accomplished without any damage (fig. 3-5A). Time the frequency and height of the swells that cover the spot. When a large enough swell is about to wash over the landing place, paddle hard on the back of the swell, so that there is water covering the surface of rocks as the kayak arrives over the chosen spot (fig. 3-5B). The idea is to plant the kayak down gently as the water subsides and then jump out of the kayak quickly and pull it out of harm's way before any following swells surge up over the rock and wash the kayak off (fig. 3-5C). Like most advanced skills, the seal landing is best practiced in controlled conditions. Choose a time when the swells rise up gently over flat rocks that are protected by a good covering of weed. Success in conditions such as these will give you confidence to attempt a seal landing when the sea and the rocks are less inviting and the urgency is greater.

Strokes and Braces

Forward Stroke

A competent sea kayaker should be able to paddle at an average speed of 3 to 4 knots. This is especially necessary if any sort of progress is to be made in adverse tidal streams. But to maintain a steady speed over many miles it is important to cultivate a good, productive, and economical style of paddling. A well-executed forward stroke will accomplish this.

Stretch the arm out and place the blade into the water well out in front of you, without making a splash. Curve the spine forward. The whole body will help pull the blade back but to do this you must swing the shoulders from the waist. The pushing hand does not cross over the center line of the kayak. As the right arm pulls back, the right foot will press on the footrest and as the left arm pulls back, the left foot will press, and so on. For a

3-5. The seal landing enables a kayaker to land on rock formations.

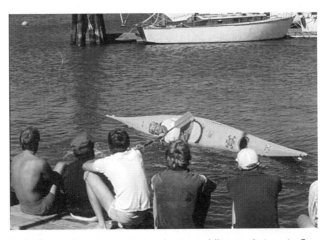

3-6. The author demonstrates basic paddling technique in San Francisco Bay. He is showing that it is possible to lean a kayak right over without getting one's hair wet. (Photo courtesy Ian Wilson)

fast stroke in calm weather, keep the paddle blades close to the side of the kayak. In rough seas or high winds allow the paddle to sweep farther out to the side. With a straight-keeled sea kayak this should not affect the boat's directional stability to any extent. By slightly angling the upper edge of the submerged paddle toward the stern, you will find that the moving blade both gives support and propels you forward. If the wind and waves are on the beam or are quartering aft (i.e., coming from the stern and about 45 degrees to the side), the tendency will be for the kayak to swing around (usually it will be the bow that will try and point into the wind). Novices tend to correct this by paddling harder on one side than the other. Over many miles this can be tiring and unpleasant. There is a better way.

Suppose the high wind is on your right side (starboard). Lean your boat over onto its right side. The curve of the hull's waterline is now in the position of a keel. This will cause the kayak to cut a slightly curved track through the water. To hold the boat in this position, brace your upper or left knee under the cockpit coaming and straighten the lower or right leg. The deck of the boat is now correctly presented to any waves breaking on the beam. This position can be maintained comfortably for many miles. To counteract any sudden swing around, you should sweep out as far as you can by straightening out your right arm. Increase the supporting angle of the blade and push yourself back on track by an extra vigorous sweep while leaning the kayak a little farther over. Practice this in calm water before trying it on the open sea.

Sweep Stroke

The sweep stroke is a simple way of turning a kayak or correcting direction when your kayak is not running straight.

To execute a sweep stroke reach well forward and place the paddle blade into the water close to

the side of the hull with the driving face outward and the top edge of the blade angled slightly in the direction of the sweep. You should be braced firmly in the cockpit. Sweep the paddle outward and back with the whole blade submerged so that it travels in a semicircle. Allow the kayak to lean over toward the paddle, which is pushed out as far as possible from the side. The stroke will finish with the paddle near the stern. Because the kayak leans over onto the gunwale, it will turn much easier than if in an upright position. As the paddle nears the stern, allow the boat to come upright again. The kayak will be supported only so long as the angled blade is moving. In strong winds or rough seas, the paddle may be held in the extended position in order to gain better leverage.

To turn the kayak, execute a reverse sweep (fig. 3-7) on one side and a forward sweep (fig. 3-8) on the other. The paddle blade should be just below the surface, the arm reaching out fully extended, and the elbow slightly bent. If the paddle blade is angled to give maximum support during the sweep, the kayak can be leaned well over, thus gaining an advantage from its width amidships and thereby giving the long straight-keeled sea kayak a false rocker upon which to turn.

In beam seas created by high winds, it is sometimes easier to perform three or four strong reverse sweep strokes, leaning the boat and allowing the wind to help blow you around in order to start the boat moving. If the sweep stokes are timed carefully, the approaching waves can be used to pivot the boat, thus making the turn much easier.

Draw Stroke

The draw stroke (fig. 3-9) is important for the quick positioning of boats during deep-water rescues and is often vital during Eskimo rescues. It should be done with determination so that kayaks can be positioned regardless of any chop on the

3-9. The draw stroke helps a kayaker position himself during rescues.

3-7. The reverse sweep stroke

3-8. The forward sweep stroke

surface of the sea. Every second counts, especially with an Eskimo rescue, but it takes strength to move a long kayak sideways against a beam wind. On the other hand, if the stroke is helped by a high wind it is all too easy for the boat to overrun the paddle blade, which can cause a capsize.

To execute the draw stroke, extend the paddle out over the side in the direction you wish to move and fully submerge the blade. Pivoting somewhere near the center of the paddle shaft, pull the driving face of the paddle blade toward you with your lower arm and push the other blade away from you with your upper arm until the paddle is nearly vertical. Then twist the shaft so the blades turn 90 degrees. Again pivoting near the center of the paddle shaft, push the submerged blade away from you with your lower arm and pull the upper blade toward you with your upper arm until the paddle is back to the starting position. During the entire operation the lower blade should be submerged at a constant depth.

Sculling for Support Stroke

The sculling for support stroke will either hold you level with the surface of the water or scull you back into the upright position again. The stroke can be performed with the paddle held in either the normal or extended paddling position. In figure 3-10 the paddler has capsized with a fully loaded reardeck. The air inside this equipment together with the buoyancy aid may prevent her from capsizing completely.

Move the paddle, which has been extended as shown in figure 3-10, to and fro in a small arc. During the movement, keep the leading edge of

3-10. Sculling for support

3-11. The stern rudder is a steering stroke used to correct directional instability caused by a following sea.

the blade high. At the point where the blade changes direction, raise the trailing edge of the blade to create a new leading edge. In this way the paddle planes just below the surface and supports you or raises you into the upright position.

Stern Rudder

The stern rudder (fig. 3-11) is primarily a steering stroke, and its main application in sea kayaking is to correct any directional instability caused by a following sea, whether it is inshore surf or on the open ocean. A following sea (when the waves approach from the rear) can be difficult to handle because if the waves are large enough, the kayak will surf forward.

For this stroke place the paddle in the water vertically, about a foot out from the side toward the stern. The back of the blade faces outward. To apply the stroke, push the blade out and away from the side while the boat is moving forward. The boat will turn on that side.

There is a procedure for coping with a following sea so that energy can be used economically and the danger of a capsize minimized. After a kayak has been overtaken by a wave, it will be

retarded in the trough. At this stage, ease off the forward paddle stroke and increase to full effort only when the next wave has caught up with the paddler and the kayak is again surging forward on the face of the wave (see fig. 3-13, p. 43). If you are inexperienced, this can be a little alarming. To combat any instability, the paddle shaft can be twisted so that the back of the blade is trailed almost flat on the surface of the water behind the paddler. If the boat tends to swing around away from the paddle stroke, you must change the paddle support over to that side quickly in order to have continued stability.

Paddle Brace

The paddle brace (fig. 3-12) is one of the most important of all sea kayaking techniques; it is this technique that enables a paddler to remain upright while beaming onto a breaking wave. When you apply a paddle brace, it is important that you fit snugly in the cockpit and are able to grip the underside of the cockpit coaming with your knees. If you are a slack fit, you will be plucked out of the cockpit and left bracing on the wave while the kayak goes bouncing to shore without you.

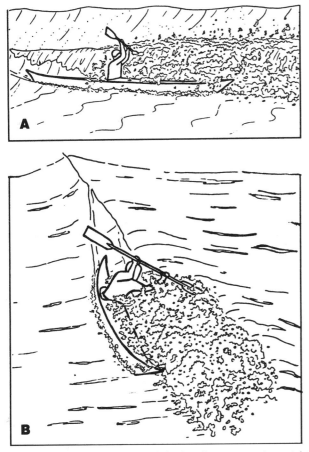

3-12. The paddle brace enables the kayaker to remain upright while beam onto a large (A) or small (B) breaking wave.

The paddle brace is used mainly for landing through surf, playing in surf, or running before steep following waves out on the open sea.

To execute the paddle brace on a large wave (fig. 3-12A) lean your kayak well over into the breaking wave, throwing your weight on the downward driving face of the paddle. You must place the paddle into the face of the toppling wave or as high as possible into the foam.

To execute the paddle brace on a small breaking wave (fig. 3-12B), place the paddle on top and just a little behind the wave with the driving face of the paddle downward. The blade will be sup-ported on the upsurge of water inside the wave, but you must lean over into the oncoming wave to maintain the brace; if not, you will capsize with considerable violence in the direction the wave is traveling.

Handling Waves

Paddling over waves of one sort or another is what kayaking on the ocean is all about. Without waves the sport we love would be dreary and dull. It is waves, however, that cause novices many of their problems, so it is perhaps as well if we look at these sometimes perplexing water patterns.

Waves come in various shapes and sizes, ranging from mild ripples to what appear to be skyscraping nightmares. As you sit out on the open sea, the first thing you will be aware of is the ground swell. I once heard this likened to a mouse crawling underneath a sheet. The sheet rises up as the lump passes beneath it, then the surface falls back into the same place again. This is what happens to the surface of the sea. As the swell passes and moves onward on its ponderous way to its ultimate destination, anything floating on the surface of the ocean will settle back again into almost the same position it was in before the swell passed beneath it. Because of this, the largest deep-water swell is quite harmless to the ocean paddler. Remember, however, that you may eventually have to land, and majestic, awe-inspiring swells can create frighteningly dangerous surf. Old swell patterns can be complicated by more recent swells coming from a different angle, or even from a different direction altogether.

To add to the confusion, a strong wind may whip up steep seas from yet another direction, and reflected waves from a pier, breakwater, or cliff can confuse the pattern even further. The newcomer to ocean kayaking will probably find this all bewildering, and only experience will bring confidence.

Following Sea

To the experienced paddler on open waters, the following sea is a free ticket. As he surfs forward, covering many miles with ease, his only problem may be to avoid cutting into the side or ramming the rear end of one of his companions. For the leader who tows a tired group member, the danger of a following sea is that the exhausted person may collide with or overrun the person towing.

A following sea causes the waves most feared by the inexperienced paddler, who would much rather be paddling into them. As the waves come from behind, they catch up with the unfortunate novice. The angle of his kayak tilts forward, he becomes unstable, and gets the impression—usually a correct one—that he is being thrown forward fast and is out of control. As the kayak is thrust forward, the wave will cause it to swing around and broach and this can all too easily cause a capsize. (For the remedy see discussion of the stern rudder, fig. 3-11, p. 40.)

Although a following sea can give an easy ride to the experienced paddler, it is easy to waste energy by attempting to paddle when your kayak is in the wrong position on the wave.

In Figure 3-13, the paddler feels the wave surge him forward (fig. 3-13A), and he increases the strength of his paddle stroke to get the maxi-

---

One day as we were out fishing in still, calm weather, the sky suddenly darkened to the south. We knew the wind was coming, and gathered up our lines with all haste. But before we were ready the storm was upon us, first with a few preparatory gusts, and then in all its wild fury. The sea flew black and white before it, the calm surface was soon one sheet of foam. The current and the wind met here; the green waves broke in crests of white spray, and the canoes were lost to each other in the hollows. We had to make for shore to save our fish and ourselves, and we paddled away as fast as we could go with the sea on our beam....

... You have to keep a sharp eye on these big breaking seas, for if one of them catches the canoe before the paddle is well out on the leeside there is every chance of its occupant going to the bottom for ever and a day.

When we reached the shore we kept along it under shelter. Then we ran northwards fast; before the wind, and now the "kayak" was even harder to manage than before. The big seas came rolling up from behind, and it was no easy matter to keep an even keel. As the wave comes you give a couple of powerful strokes and let the paddle float out to the side. Then the stern is lifted high in the air and you lean hard back. As the wave breaks you feel a heavy blow on the back, while the spray showers round you, and you seem to fly through space on the foaming crest. Then it rolls by you, you sink into the hollow, and with a few more vigorous strokes you ride again on the back of the next wave.

I had a good companion and instructor in Eliase, who kept the whole time as close to my side as the sea would let him. Now he would shoot past me on the top of one wave, and then I would ride by him on the next. It was a dance with the waves and a game with danger.

Presently the shore turned westwards and again offered us shelter. But first there was a belt of ice to pass, and it was necessary to bring the canoes through without getting them crushed between the moving floes. We found an opening and seized the opportunity, and with a few quick strokes sailed through on the top of the sea. (Nansen, The First Crossing of Greenland, pp. 422–24.)

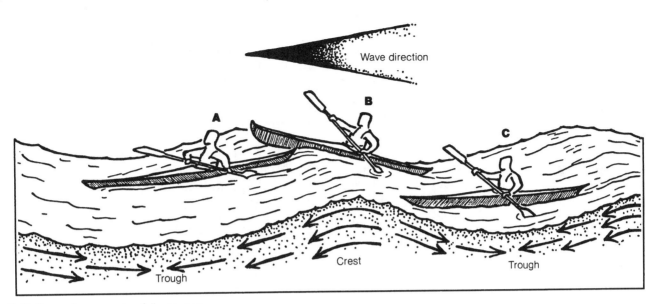

Wave direction

A

B

C

Trough

Crest

Trough

3-13. Conserving energy in a following sea

mum amount from its effect on his boat. As he moves quickly down the face of the wave, he executes a stern rudder on his left-hand side, thus keeping himself on track.

The wave passes beneath the paddler (fig. 3-13B) and he immediately feels the retarding effect of his position on the back of the wave crest. This is the time when he should ease off the strength of his stroke until the next swell catches up with him.

In the trough (fig. 3-13C), the paddler is almost standing still. As he feels the stern lift, however, he should increase the strength of his paddle stroke. The angle of his kayak will increase as the face of the wave rises under him, and he will begin to surf forward.

If you are a novice and unsure of your balance, do not increase the strength of your paddle stroke when you feel your stern rise as in figure 3-13C. In this way, you will not allow your kayak to reach "surf velocity" (speed of the wave). If the waves are steep and perhaps—to your horror—curling over at the crest, take great care. As the stern of the kayak lifts to the wave, give a couple

of reverse strokes to act as a brake and thus prevent the kayak from reaching surfing speed against your wishes.

Beam Sea

In a beam sea, the waves come from the side, giving novices the feeling that they are going to be bowled over sideways. In situations like this, lean gently into the waves and as you paddle forward, angle the top of your rearward traveling blade slightly toward the stern. In this way the blade is giving you support as well as propulsion. At the end of the stroke, when the paddle blade is at the rear and the driving face is almost tilted upward, you may find it necessary to support yourself. Do this by trailing the back of the blade along the surface of the water in the low brace position as a wave breaks over your gunwale.

Large breaking beam seas are best dealt with by employing a paddle brace. If a large wave catches you out and breaks over you, at the very moment when the paddle blade on that side is halfway through a forward paddle stroke, it may be necessary to flick the rear traveling blade over into the high brace support position (see fig. 3-12, p. 41).

Head Sea

Paddling into oncoming seas on a moderately calm day is pleasant for novice and expert alike. The novice gets a feeling of stability, and even seasoned paddlers have the sensation of traveling over the water much faster than they really are. If, however, these approaching seas are caused by a high wind, it often takes determination and strength to battle against them. Even though the waves may be small, the wind will drain your strength and, what is more important, your will and morale. Remember, keep calm and keep your head down. You will move forward slowly, even into the teeth of gale-force winds.

When an ocean swell travels into shallow water, the bottom drag causes the wave to slow down. This means that the wave in deeper water will catch up. When this happens we say that the wavelength, or the distance between the wave crests, has become shorter. The nearer a wave gets to the shore, the steeper it becomes. The wave following behind is always in deeper water, but its distance to the wave in front is always getting shorter. Due to the decreased wavelength, the leading wave will become unstable, whereupon it will topple over and break.

A breaking wave can take two main forms. It can either plunge or spill.

Plunging, or Dumping, Waves

These occur when an approaching swell meets a shore that is steeply sloping. All goes well until the wave reaches a point where its depth is about equal to its height. As soon as that point is reached, the wave will overbalance forward, topple over, and break with an explosive release of energy, usually mingled with pebbles, sand, and grit, and

sometimes even large logs! It is the crushing force of these dumping waves that causes kayakers so much concern during landings and launchings from steeply angled beaches (see p. 36).

Spilling Waves

This is the kind of wave beloved of surfers. As the swell approaches a gently sloping beach, the wave will start to break gradually in water approximately twice as deep as it is high. At this point, the wave crest will tumble over and spill down the face of the wave. Because it lacks the violence of the dumper, this type of wave is quite manageable to anyone paddling inshore with a landing in mind—so long as the usual surf techniques are applied when appropriate (see Stern Rudder and Paddle Brace, pp. 40-41).

Refraction

Waves sometimes bend when they begin to slow down upon reaching shallow water. This is known as refraction. In figure 3-14 the approaching waves are affected by the breakwater. The part of the wave closest to the obstacle will be the first affected by the shallow water. This will slow down that end of the wave. The effect is rather like that of a rank of marching soldiers turning a corner; the inside men march on the spot, while the outside men maintain their speed and pace and swing around. As the waves bend, they also lose height, so whereas the breaking waves at A are quite violent, those at B will be much more manageable, and a trouble-free landing could probably be made at C. The surf at D is getting increasingly larger and more intimidating.

Figure 3-15 shows the behavior of a swell traveling along a shoreline. The side of the headland at A is receiving the main force of the waves, making landings difficult in all but the calmest conditions. The best place for a landing will be at

3-14. Refraction

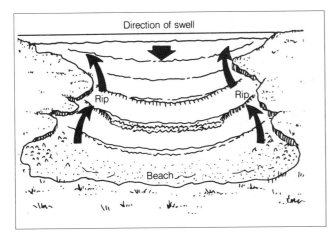

3-16. Refraction of swell in a small bay

B where the shallow water causes the wave to refract and reduce in size. A landing at C might be possible, but coming ashore at D would be dangerous.

Bays usually provide good landing conditions and excellent places to go surfing. Figure 3-16 shows what happens when an ocean swell enters a small bay. The largest surf is in the middle, but because of refraction, the size of the waves diminishes toward the sides. Water is drained back out to sea by rips. These rips will also help flatten down the surf, making these areas good for a dry launching and an almost surf-free landing.

Refraction around an Island

In figure 3-17 an ocean swell is approaching a small island or a rocky islet close inshore. The waves are influenced by the presence of the land-mass, so they are refracted and bend around the island in the manner shown. Beyond the island the swells converge, and here standing waves of varying severity are formed.

Close to the island at A, the waves will be small. At position B the angle of the meeting waves may cause peaks to form in a manner similar to that illustrated. Farther away from the island at C, the angle of approach is much more acute due to the refraction of the wave. It is in this area that clapotis may occur (see below). When seeking shelter or a landing in the lee of an island therefore, this area should be approached with caution. Shallow water will increase the severity of any breaking seas.

Clapotis

In figure 3-18 the waves are striking the sea wall at a much more acute angle or perhaps even parallel to it. The wave is once again reflected, but instead of crossing the wave pattern at right angles, it rebounds and collides head on with the

3-17. This illustration demonstrates wave refraction around an island. Some reflected waves may be caused at A. The danger spot is at B where the converging waves can cause "clapotis." The height of the waves C will begin to decrease.

3-18. Clapotis occurs as: A. An incoming swell surges up side of sea wall. B. A huge amount of water falls back away from wall. C. A returning swell speeds seaward. D. Incoming swell collides with outgoing "C," which creates explosive "clapotis," sending water high into the air.

3-19. Reflection occurs when a swell meets an obstruction such as a sea wall or a vertical cliff.

next oncoming wall of water. The result, which is frighteningly powerful and explosive, is known as clapotis.

This is not an area in which to play, unless you like living dangerously and the boat you are paddling belongs to someone else. I once sat only a few yards from a man who was attempting to see how close he could get to the area of clapotis without getting wet. Unfortunately, due to a slight miscalculation on his part, to his horror and great fright, his world exploded beneath him. He proceeded skyward to a height of about 20 feet. The rescue was made in calm water only 20 yards or so from the danger area.

Reflection

In figure 3-19 the waves, generated by a swell, are approaching the sea wall at an angle only slightly less than ninety degrees. After coming into contact with the solid obstruction, the waves reflect off, converge, and are superimposed at right angles to the original wave pattern. When a crest meets a crest, the peak so formed will be higher than the original wave.

For the experienced kayaker, paddling in this rebound area can be an exhilarating experience. One moment the boat drops into a trough, the next it is picked up to pirouette on a pyramid of water. This is also an ideal area for advanced training. In the event of a capsize, however, and before a rescue is attempted, the swimmer should tow his boat and paddle out of the immediate vicinity of any breaking seas.

Even in the absence of any swell, I find that one of the most tiring seas is the short reflected chop caused by an onshore wind against a steep or rocky coastline. The small, bouncy reflected waves cause a kayak to twist about seemingly with a mind of its own. With boring monotony, every other stroke or so has to be accompanied by a corrective lean and sweep. Fortunately, the advent of drop-down skegs has helped to reduce this problem.

You cannot rank as an expert kaiak-man until you have mastered the art of righting yourself after capsizing. To do this, you seize one end of the paddle in your hand, and with the other hand grasp the shaft as near the middle as possible; then you place it along the side of the kaiak with its free end pointing forward towards the bow; and thereupon, pushing the end of the paddle sharply out to the side, and bending your body well forward towards the deck, you raise yourself by a strong circular sweep of the paddle.

If you do not come right up, a second stroke may be necessary.

A thorough kaiak-man can also right himself without an oar by help of his throwing-stick, or even without it, by means of one arm. The height of accomplishment is reached when he does not even need to use the flat of his hand, but can clench it; and to show that he really does so, I have seen a man take a stone in his clenched hand before capsizing, and come up with it still in his grasp. (Nansen, Eskimo Life, *pp. 52–53.)*

THE ESKIMO ROLL
AND OTHER SELF-RESCUES

What was once a survival technique used by the Eskimo kayak hunters of the Arctic is now the normal way in which modern sea kayakers right themselves after an accidental capsize. Not everyone who paddles a kayak can Eskimo roll and not everyone wants to learn how to do it. It is, however, an easily mastered skill, especially if you are taught in the warm, pampering confines of a swimming pool by someone who knows what he is doing and can correct your mistakes while you are hanging upside down and worrying yourself to death.

Of all the different types of Eskimo rolls—and I teach ten methods to my students—I consider the screw roll the quickest and best in a survival situation. It can be performed without changing the hand position on the paddle, and because the paddle is not used in an extended manner as with some rolls, there is less chance of straining the shaft or snapping a blade.

Screw Roll

The screw roll is so called because while moving forward, the paddler appears to screw himself

4-1. This Eskimo roll in the cold waters of the North Sea off the Farne Islands shows that the paddler doesn't mind cold water. (Photo courtesy Kieth Morris)

around and through the water without any break in the paddle stroke (see fig. 4-2).

If you think you are going to capsize, breathe in enough air to last you out and keep calm; a panicky paddler will not hold his breath for long. If the water is cold, be prepared for the shock of its icy fingers gripping your temples and taking your breath away.

4-2. Surface view of the screw roll

As soon as you are upside down, you must get into the "wind-up" (pronounced "wynd") or surface preparatory position for starting the roll (fig. 4-2A). Push your head and arms up toward the surface and the light. Assuming that you are right-handed, the angle of the oval paddle shaft, as you feel it in your left hand, will indicate to you the angle of the forward paddle blade (fig. 4-2B). (If you practice this on dry land with your eyes shut, it will help consolidate the movement and the hand positions in your mind.)

Push the right hand out from the side of the hull. At the same time, push the left hand up high enough to let the rear blade miss the hull of the upturned boat and allow the forward blade to sweep right around until it is at right angles to the kayak (figs. 4-2C and D).

If you hold the forward blade at the correct angle—that is with its leading edge high as it sweeps out—it will plane along the surface of the water, supporting you and lifting you toward the surface. The secret is to sweep out until your right bicep touches your nose. As it does so, jerk your right hand down violently, giving a small push upward with the left hand, and simultaneously flick your hips (fig. 4-2E).

During the roll, the left foot should be pressing against the footrest and your knees should be spread apart so that they grip the underside of the cockpit coaming. If you do not do this, you will pull yourself right out of the kayak like a cork from a bottle. Some people find that leaning backward until their head almost touches the reardeck helps them roll more easily.

In figure 4-3 the paddler is sitting ready in the wind-up position. Throughout the roll, the hands must retain their normal grip on the paddle. Consequently, when the wind-up position is adopted, the wrists must be bent down as far as possible. To fully appreciate the movement of the paddle during the roll, turn this book upside down and view the illustration in the inverted position.

Note: The front blade has its driving force upwards, while the outer and leading edge is angled slightly down toward the water. Once you are capsized, this paddle position will ensure that the outward sweep has a surface-planing action. It will also help if you twist your body through ninety degrees before pushing the head and arms up to the light, prior to the outward sweep.

Some people find it advantageous to practice the paddle movement standing on land without the kayak. The push up to the surface can be simulated by bending down at the waist. In this way, beginners can become used to the movements that their bodies and arms must perform, without the inhibiting effect of water up the nose.

Fish Eye View

Surface View

4-3. This is a movement diagram of the screw roll.

During practice in warm, safe water, wear a noseclip. Hanging upside down with one half of your body in the water and the other half above water does your sinus cavities no good at all.

Do not let rolling a kayak full of equipment worry you. You will find that a fully loaded boat rolls just as easily as an empty one. The only time you will have a problem is if the reardeck has been used to carry a quantity of bulky equipment. You will find that the difficulty is not in rolling but in capsizing completely so that a 360-degree roll may be performed. This will depend to a large extent upon the amount of air trapped inside what you carry, which forces the kayak to lie on its side and stay there. If this happens, forget the roll, just scull up with the paddle on that side.

Remember, to master the Eskimo roll is a sign of success, but to have to roll is a sign of failure. And, of course, just as you are about to break the surface, after what you consider to have been a textbook roll, your paddle shaft may snap.

Broken Paddle

In figure 4-4 the paddler had been attempting a Pawlata roll only to have the shaft of her paddle snap off completely.

Breaking a paddle in the act of rolling could be classified as one of life's little catastrophes. All is not lost, however, and you still might come through without having to swim. An Eskimo faced with the same problem would probably try to roll up using the throwing stick from his harpoon or even his knife. You will not have a throwing stick, but you should have one half of the paddle left in your hand. Do not panic and drop it.

Here is what you do (see fig. 4-5): Keep calm. Wrap your right hand around the edge of the paddle blade near the center (fig. 4-5A). Lean back so that your head is touching the reardeck. Hold the blade so that your palm is facing outward and your knuckles are against your left ear. Extend your left arm out at a right angle to the boat, palm

4-4. A broken paddle during an attempted roll

down, fingers slightly apart but not fully open. Twist your head up toward the light on that (left) side. Strike down violently with your left hand, keeping the arm straight as it approaches position X (that is the limit of the left hand's effectiveness). Your right hand will now follow the path of the left hand by striking out and down with the paddle blade.

As the blade on its downward sweep passes the left hand (fig. 4-5B), throw the left hand over violently in the direction of the solid arrow (fig. 4-5C). This acts as a counterbalance and helps the kayak to flick over and complete the roll (fig. 4-5D).

Throughout this whole maneuver, *your head must remain touching the reardeck. If your head moves away you won't come up.* To practice the amount of sweep needed and the sequence of left and right hands, stand with your back and head touching a wall, your arms in position. At the start of the righthand sweep, the fingertips will be touching the wall, knuckles touching the left ear. At the end of the sweep, the palm of the right hand will be flat against the wall on the right side. Remember, when you are in the kayak you must keep your head on the reardeck while twisting your hips and body in the direction opposite to the thrust of the paddle blade.

If you wish to take this maneuver even further, gradually reduce the size of the blade area held in the right hand and you will finish up performing a hand roll. To gain extra surface pressure from your hand alone, open the fingers slightly.

4-5. Recovering after breaking a paddle while rolling

Headstand

Although the headstand was first publicized in Germany in the mid-1930s as part of some rolling instructions, it is not strictly speaking a roll but more a support stroke: you go over and come up on the same side. Unlike the sculling for support stroke, the headstand is one that can be done from a completely inverted position and is for those whose rolling capabilities are perhaps a little suspect or who find themselves lying on the surface of the water with a fully loaded reardeck. This is especially so for those who find themselves capsized on their "wrong" rolling side (i.e., on their left side if they are right-handed or on their right side if they are left-handed).

Figure 4-6 shows how to capsize on the right-hand side. As you capsize, let the right blade slice down, bringing the left one over. While this is happening, change your hand position (fig. 4-6A). Let go of the shaft with your left hand and grasp the lower blade, fingers outward. Turn your right hand over on the paddle shaft so that your palm is facing outward (fig. 4-6B). Once you are completely upside down, twist your body sideways and allow your chest and shoulders to rise parallel to the surface of the water. If you are in clear, shallow water, the bottom should be directly facing you. Place the paddle shaft over your right shoulder so that the blade is sticking straight up into fresh air. The palm of your right hand is still facing outward. To raise yourself to the surface, strike the paddle down violently with your right hand (fig. 4-6C). As the extended paddle strikes the water, lift the near blade with your left hand. As your body breaks the surface, flick your hips (fig. 4-6D).

Paddling Alone

Paddling alone on the sea is dangerous, but if you must, take certain precautions:
- You should be able to do an Eskimo roll on the first try.
- You should be suitably dressed for immersion.
- You should fit your kayak with either watertight hatches, bulkheads, and a bilge pump; a pod; or flotation material or inflatable buoyancy that fills the boat fore and aft to capacity

4-6. The headstand can be done in place of a roll when capsizing.

and is securely fixed in position and tailored to the shape of the kayak. A plastic cup or bailer should be attached to a string.

- You should use a paddle leash in difficult conditions.
- You should take normal safety precautions (flares, a PFD, notifying the Coast Guard of your plans).
- You should perfect a method of self-rescue that can be performed in rough conditions in the event a roll is unsuccessful.

Self-Rescues

In the event of a capsize, the first thing to do is remove yourself from the conditions that capsized you. If your boat is inside the surf line and it is too dangerous to swim in, tow your kayak well outside the area. Swimming at right angles to an overfall or tide race should get you out of it and into water that is a little calmer.

Reentry and Roll

The reentry and roll is an unassisted self-rescue for the lone paddler who for some reason finds herself in the water, out of her kayak, and alone.

Position the kayak so that the bow is pointing toward any oncoming waves. Face the stern and hold both sides of the cockpit coaming (fig. 4-7A). Hold the paddle on the side you are used to for rolling. If you have been paddling alone, you should be wearing a paddle leash. Relax and take a deep breath. Throw your head backward and down and bring your legs up and into the cockpit (fig. 4-7B). In a practice session when you are not wearing a buoyancy aid, you will find that you finish up in the seat after a simple, underwater back somersault. A buoyancy aid will float you up on one side during reentry, however, and this could

confuse you. You must maintain a firm grip on the cockpit coaming so the kayak maintains its position in relation to you as you enter. Roll up. If you are without bulkheads, hatches, or a pump, balance carefully and replace the spray cover. Open the waist elastic to gain access to the cockpit area, then start bailing. Support yourself by placing the paddle across your shoulders and sculling. This is hard work, but the larger the bailer the less time it takes.

If you are carrying a paddle float, you could put it on the end of the paddle to give support, as an alternative to sculling.

With bulkheads, hatches, and pump, balance carefully, replace the spray cover, and start pumping. You may have to rest the paddle across your shoulders and scull for support (fig. 4-8). If your kayak is fitted with a pod—or a device that acts in a similar manner—you need to paddle into calmer water, mop out whatever little water has entered your cockpit area, and then replace your spray cover.

4-7. The reentry and roll is an unassisted self-rescue.

4-8. Sculling for support while pumping

In rough seas, the spray cover must be in place before emptying starts, otherwise the kayak will fill up again as fast as you get the water out. The spray cover must be large enough around the waist to allow the paddler to bail through it. This adaptation to the cover is one you may have to do yourself. You must be able to get the bailer down between your knees if you hope to get any water out, so don't make the bailer too large.

Paddle Float

Novices should not paddle out into open water alone. When the water is smooth and unruffled and the air is warm, however, the temptation can be irresistible, and people will go out unaccompanied despite advice to the contrary.

The novice who capsizes will probably not attempt an Eskimo roll. An underwater reentry will not be part of his repertoire. In a book of this nature, I feel there should be a description of at least one solo rescue that a frightened novice can attempt with a reasonable chance of success.

The paddle float is not meant for rough seas, and although I have seen experienced kayakers succeed in rough conditions, this was due more to their experience and perseverance. This rescue is for the unpracticed paddler who is overbalanced

by a gust of wind or capsizes for some other reason on calm water.

The method originated in Europe. When it was first described, however, it was not taken seriously by sea paddlers. In this method, some means of portable flotation is fastened to the end of the paddle, which is then used as an outrigger. The original suggestion, that one's life jacket should be removed and secured to the end of the paddle, was greeted with only a small amount of enthusiasm. Because reentry can be performed by a lone paddler, however, it was not completely discarded.

The method was refined on the West Coast of the United States by substituting a plastic water container for the life jacket. Thus, removing one's protection was no longer necessary. Unfortunately, the novice still had to fiddle with knots in order to tie the float to the paddle, which is not the sort of exercise that a frightened novice needs. The system was improved further by Will Nordby of California. After a frightening capsize, he experimented with various airfilled floats and cushions to see if it was possible to make the paddle float easier to use. He and his friend Bob Licht of Sea Trek got together to design and market the first "paddle float" (fig. 4-9).

This paddle float is simply a soft, strong plastic bag, and because the walls of the bag have an inner and outer skin, they can be inflated by mouth. The paddle float takes up little room, and for safety's sake it can be carried in a pocket on the life jacket. Once the float is slid over the end of the paddle blade and inflated, it cannot be removed until the air is let out again.

Before attempting to use the paddle float, make sure you have strong shock cord elastics fitted in a position that suits you (either on the fore- or reardeck) so that the paddle is held firmly in place.

In the event of a capsize, bail out and quickly right the kayak. Push the paddle through the deck elastics *before* you fit the paddle float. Position

4-9. The paddle float (Photo courtesy Will Nordby)

4-10. A self-rescue with a paddle float is an easy way for a novice to reenter the boat in calm water.

yourself on the downwind side of the boat while inflating the float so that you do not lose contact with your kayak. Twist the outer paddle blade so that it lies flat on the surface of the water. Hoist your body up and onto the reardeck and hook your foot over the paddle (fig. 4-10A). Keep your weight on the float side and place the leading foot into the cockpit (fig. 4-10B). At the same time, shift the trailing foot onto the loom. Then move the trailing foot into the cockpit and slide both legs toward the bow (fig. 4-10C). Rotate your body forward while keeping your weight toward the float side (fig. 4-10D).

My advice to any frightened beginner who feels incapable of tackling this procedure is to spend time learning the Eskimo roll or cultivating a faithful companion.

DEEP-WATER RESCUES

Once you have decided that you are going to paddle a kayak, whether on the ocean, a lake, or a river, you may as well resign yourself to the fact that during the early learning stages, a few capsizes are to be expected. When you get better and more experienced, you become more adventurous and more willing to paddle in rough conditions, so there is always a chance of inadvertently becoming a swimmer. The best remedy for a capsize is undoubtedly the Eskimo roll. Not everyone can or wants to Eskimo roll, however, and some kayaks are almost impossible to roll due to excessive beam or an inhibiting deck design. To overcome these problems, various methods have been developed over the years for emptying capsized kayaks and then putting the owners safely back into them. The water does not have to be very deep to merit this type of emergency procedure; in fact, water up to the eyeballs is just about right for a deep-water rescue.

Since I began kayaking on the sea, I have watched with humor, and sometimes horror, many rescue methods tried with varying degrees of success. I have observed group rescues with as many as six people working out a complicated rescue sequence involving an ingenious system of levers

and pulleys brought about by the careful positioning of kayaks and paddles. I have observed solo rescues with a purple-faced man desperately trying to tread water in a rough sea while, at the same time, blowing down a large U-shaped tube inserted into his inverted cockpit, all in an effort to expel the water and raise the kayak. Needless to say, neither of these methods achieved widespread popularity.

The methods of rescue and reentry that follow should all be practiced in the calm waters of a sheltered bay or a swimming pool. It can be dangerous to practice under very cold or rough conditions.

Remember that it is vital that a capsized paddler maintain a firm hold on the kayak at all times, even if this means doing so during the bail-out underwater. It is good to remember that even though initial practices may be on placid water where the upturned kayak stays in one place, in an open-water situation things might be very different, and the upturned kayak could be blown away faster than the capsized kayaker can swim after it. If your paddle drifts away during a rescue, always swim the kayak to the paddle. In windy weather, *never leave the kayak in order to swim to the paddle*. You can retrieve it later.

After a rescue practice, the surface of the sea

The author cresting a wave six miles out to sea. (Photo courtesy Martin Melig)

. . . A kaiak-man who has entirely mastered the art of righting himself can defy almost any weather. If he is capsized, he is on even keel again in a moment, and can play like a sea-bird with the waves, and cut right through them. If the sea is very heavy, he lays the broadside of his kaiak to it, holds the paddle flat out on the windward side, pressing it against the deck, bends forward, and lets the wave roll over him; or else he throws himself on his side towards it, resting on his flat paddle, and rights himself again when it has passed. The prettiest feat of seamanship I have ever heard of is that to which some fishers, I am told, have recourse among overwhelming rollers. As the sea curls down over them they voluntarily capsize, receive it on the bottom of the kaiak, and when it has passed right themselves again. I think it would be difficult to name a more intrepid method of dealing with a heavy sea. (Nansen, Eskimo Life, p. 54.)

should not be littered with floating debris such as flare containers, lunch box, the contents of first-aid and repair kits, or pieces of bloodstained polyethylene flotation foam.

As you become more proficient, by all means progress to rougher water, but remember that it is *always* dangerous to perform any deep-water rescue inshore to breaking surf. In this sort of situation it is far safer to tow both paddler and kayak out of the danger area, whether it is amidst waves breaking against rocks or in a tidal overfall. Rough-water practice is always made safer by wearing crash helmets.

Group leaders will soon find that one capsize can be infectious. Others follow suit and attention may be divided between two or more calamities. Rescuers may have to neglect one of the rescues and thus lose the sense of urgency so important for getting people out of cold water or dangerous conditions as quickly as possible. Leaders may often find it necessary to use a combination of rescue techniques to solve difficult rescue situations or may invent some of their own.

The key to success is plenty of practice against the clock, in controlled, choppy situations. For example, an HI rescue (see below) can be completed in fifty to sixty seconds, after surprisingly little practice.

HI Rescue

The HI rescue is so-called because of the position adopted by the kayaks on the water (see fig. 5-1). In this rescue, the person who has capsized and is in the water is rescued by two companions. Paddlers A and C position their boats quickly, collect paddler B's paddle, and then raft up facing him. Paddler B guides the bow of his upturned kayak between the two rescue craft. Paddlers A and C now lift paddler B's kayak up and over the paddles as quickly as possible (fig. 5-1A). This is really

5-1. Lifting (A) and emptying (B) a capsized kayak during an HI rescue

more of a snatch than a lift, thus allowing only a small amount of water to enter the boat. It is worth taking care to ensure that the cockpit is clear of the water before starting to pull the kayak over the paddles. If paddlers A and C are careful, they will not damage the paddle shafts as they lift the boat over. The upturned kayak now rests and pivots on the paddles. Paddlers A and C hold the boat steady. As paddler B seesaws his end of the kayak up and down, the water drains out (fig. 5-1B). As soon as the boat is empty, the two rescuers turn it over into its upright position, slide it forward off the paddles, and pull the boat back between their two kayaks. The kayak is now in a position for paddler B to reenter by one of the methods discussed later (see p. 61).

With practice this rescue should be completed in under a minute. As mentioned previously, at no time should the paddler in the water lose contact with the two rescue crafts. In high winds, it is possible that the two rescuers and the upturned boat will be blown away faster than the person in the water can swim after them.

TX Rescue

If you choose to paddle with only one other companion, you will need to know the TX rescue (fig. 5-2). Because this can be completed successfully by only one other person, it is ideal for leaders and those in charge of inexperienced groups.

Paddler B snatches up the bow of the kayak as quickly as possible so as not to drag water into the cockpit of the capsized kayak. She then lifts the kayak across the foredeck of her own boat and pulls it until the cockpit rests near her own cockpit (fig. 5-2A).

Paddler B seesaws the kayak by leaning her own boat from side to side. Paddler A helps paddler B to control the emptying movement by holding onto the bow (fig. 5-2B). Once the boat is empty, it is turned right-side up and paddler A reenters.

Paddler B must be especially careful before starting the seesawing operation. If there is too much water in the boat to be emptied, the excess weight will crack one or both of the decks. It might be prudent to remove the worst of the water by the curl method (see fig. 5-4, p. 61) before attempting the TX.

It is also easy for paddler B to damage her spray cover as she tries to drag the partially waterlogged kayak across her own cockpit. A good idea is to wear two spray covers. Wear the older and more repaired one underneath and remove the top one before the rescue starts. It is important that B looks after both pairs of paddles; this is when a paddle leash or paddle park (see p. 15) is useful.

It is possible for two boats to raft up and empty a third, in what then becomes a rafted TX

5-2. Lifting (A) and emptying (B) a capsized kayak during a TX rescue.

rescue, but I do not consider it as efficient as the HI rescue. The HI and TX rescues have only limited success if the kayak is fully loaded.

Cleopatra's Needle

A frightening situation called Cleopatra's Needle develops when a kayak, with either too little buoyancy or badly distributed buoyancy, becomes swamped (fig. 5-3). If all the necessary precautions are taken before the trip starts, this will not happen; but it could happen to other groups that you may stumble across during the course of a gentle day's outing. On two occasions I have been able to assist complete strangers in the middle of large lakes, who have had only the point of their bows showing above the surface of the water. Not a pretty sight, but if you meet up with this it will be up to you to tell the man in the water how to empty his boat.

5-3. Cleopatra's Needle occurs when a kayak with incorrect buoyancy swamps.

5-4. The curl is a method of emptying a swamped kayak.

In the past, any method of emptying a swamped kayak was very difficult, especially for frightened people of limited strength and experience. Some research was needed and, after a great deal of experimentation, I finally arrived at a method that seems to work every time and does not require an enormous amount of energy by the person in the water. I call this method the curl.

Curl

First, maneuver the kayak to the surface. This can be done by hooking the foot under the cockpit or diving down and grabbing the coaming and lifting up. Once the boat is lying on the surface with its cockpit uppermost, the emptying can begin (see fig. 5-4). The swamped boat lies alongside paddler B's. Its deck is completely awash. Paddler A pulls himself over paddler B's foredeck as near as he can to paddler B's cockpit, without getting in the way of B's paddle, and hooks his hands under the cockpit coaming of the swamped boat, his palms uppermost.

Paddler A rests his elbows on paddler B's deck, pulls the swamped kayak toward him, and tilts the cockpit so that the water starts to drain out (fig. 5-4A). Once paddler A's elbows are jammed against the deck by the weight of his kayak, B can then increase the draining angle by leaning over and sculling for support (fig. 5-4B). Apart from making sure that the draining kayak is held firmly and perfectly level, no further effort is required on the part of A. The aim of the rescue is not to empty the kayak completely, but to remove enough water so that the boat can be handled while performing one of the rescue methods previously described.

This method of rescue does not require exceptional strength. As long as paddler A can get his kayak on its side and hold it level, the water will drain out as paddler B controls the angle of the lean.

Methods of Reentry

Figure 5-5A shows a good, safe method of reentry: The paddles are made secure as a bundle across the two outside boats, and paddlers A and C have

5-5. *Safe methods of reentry with two and three kayakers*

All-In Rescue

Weather conditions sufficient to capsize all three members of a kayaking group at the same time are bound to be absolutely horrific. Yet such weather conditions can come and go quickly. I know of at least one incident off the south coast of England in which a party of nine were hit by a bad squall. All capsized in the freak wind and came out of their boats. The storm passed as quickly as it came, but by the time a helicopter had arrived to rescue them, a number were suffering from exposure. The all-in rescue will usually work even if all the paddlers of a group have been capsized. It is based on the principle that an upturned kayak can be used to form the pivot over which to empty another. To ensure success, it is essential to practice the rescue in calm, sheltered waters or a swimming pool.

Figure 5-6 shows the beginning of a rescue and reentry involving three people. The sequence of the rescue can be applied to any number of paddlers. Paddlers A and B will perform the main rescue with kayak X. Kayak Y will serve as the pivot.

Paddler C holds on to her kayak Z and to kayak Y and looks after the paddles. If she wishes she can hold the paddles between her legs to free her arms. *On no account must she become separated from the main rescue.* Paddlers A and B hold on to the upturned cockpit coaming of kayak Y and face in opposite directions (fig. 5-6A). Paddler B lifts the bow of kayak X as high and as quickly as she can, so that the cockpit clears the water. As B does this she will automatically pull down on her right hand. Any tilting of pivot boat Y is counteracted by A, however, who is holding on to the other side of the coaming. The less buoyant flotation contained by pivot boat Y, the more important it is for both paddlers to hold it perfectly level and still; otherwise the air inside will escape and the boat will sink.

firm holds on the cockpit coaming of the inside kayak. Paddler B does not have to use a great deal of energy to get back into his kayak again, although he may feel a little undignified.

Figure 5-5B shows probably the best method of reentry involving only two people. Paddler A has one arm under the paddle shaft and is gripping the coaming with both hands. This will keep the raft stable, and as paddler B exerts his weight down onto the paddle, it will increase the stability. If paddler B needs help, A can quite easily take his left hand off the cockpit coaming and grasp B's life jacket without losing stability.

5-6. Emptying and reentering a kayak in the all-in rescue

Paddler B passes kayak X over the pivot boat Y to A, who continues taking it across until its cockpit rests on the upturned hull (fig. 5-6B).

Paddlers A and B seesaw kayak X until it is empty (fig. 5-6C). Once this is done, it is turned onto its right side and placed alongside the pivot boat. Paddler B positions herself next to her cockpit to get in first.

The reentry can be tricky in rough seas. Paddler B passes her paddle across the middle of pivot kayak Y (fig. 5-6D). To gain entry, B places her right hand at the rear of the cockpit of kayak X and in the center, while holding the paddle and the front of the cockpit coaming with her left hand. She enters the cockpit by kicking out with her feet and pushing down with her weight upon her arms. To counteract any unsteadiness caused by B's reentry, A pulls down on her end of the paddle shaft. As soon as B is secure in her boat, A's kayak can be emptied using the TX rescue, and C is finally put back in her kayak using the HI method.

The order of leaving the water is very important, and the leader has some decisions to make before the rescue commences. The most scantily dressed should hardly be the last one to leave the water, but if that person is already suffering from hypothermia and is put into her boat first, she might not be able to undertake the TX rescue.

During practice the participants should change about, so that each person becomes familiar with every part of the rescue.

Eskimo Rescues

The Eskimo rescue is based on the assistance often given by one kayak hunter to another, mainly in the Greenland area. Along these coasts it was often a practice for the paddler to lace the hem of his anorak to the wooden hoop of the cockpit coaming. This made the kayak thoroughly watertight, but it also made a quick exit impossible. In the event of a capsize and failure to roll, the unfortunate occupant had to rely on his nearest companion for assistance.

Briefly, the Eskimo rescue involves a method

Here comes a gigantic roller—they can see it shining black and white in the far distance. It towers aloft so high that the sky is almost hidden. In a moment they have stuck their paddles under the thongs on the windward side and bent their bodies forward so that the crest of the wave breaks upon their backs. For a second almost everything has disappeared; those who are further a-lee await their turn in anxiety; then the billow passes, and once more the kaiaks skim forward as before. But such a sea does not come singly; the next will be worse. They hold their paddles flat to the deck and projecting to windward, bend their bodies forward, and at the moment when the white cataract thunders down upon them they hurl themselves into its very jaws, thus somewhat breaking its force. For a moment they have again disappeared—then one kaiak comes up on even keel, and presently another appears bottom upwards. It is Pedersuak (i.e. the Big Peter) who has capsized. His comrade speeds to his side, but at the same moment the third wave breaks over them and he must look out for himself. It is too late—the two kaiaks lie heaving bottom upwards. The second manages to right himself, and his first thought is for his comrade, to whose assistance he once more hastens. He runs his kaiak alongside of the other, lays his paddle across both, bends down so that he gets hold under the water of his comrade's arm, and with a jerk drags him up upon his side, so that he too can get hold of the paddle and in an instant raise himself upon even keel. The water-tight jacket has come a little loose from the ring on one side and some water has got in; not much, however, but he can still keep afloat. The others have in the meantime come up; they get hold of the lost paddle, and all can again push forward. (Nansen, Eskimo Life, pp. 67–68.)

in which the paddler who capsizes remains in his kayak while a fellow paddler maneuvers his kayak to the upturned hull. The capsized paddler then rights himself by using any part of the rescuer's kayak or paddle that is offered.

Bow Rescue

Figure 5-7 illustrates the bow rescue. Victim B keeps calm and bangs hard and quickly on his upturned hull to attract attention. Paddler B then raises his hands high in the air above the bottom of his hull and moves them slowly backward and forward. This makes it easier for A to place the bow of the rescue boat into B's hands (fig. 5-7A).

Once A sees that B has a firm hold on the lifting toggle (or his hands clasped tightly on the bow itself), he should paddle forward gently so that the rescued kayak is held steady against B's outward push as he raises himself to the surface (fig. 5-7B).

Paddler A must paddle into the rescue at a controlled speed. Remember that B, who is submerged, could be getting nervous and may decide to surface just at the very moment that A paddles

5-7. The bow rescue

in at breakneck speed. Nobody wants a kayak up his nose at five knots. Paddler B should leave himself enough air so that if he feels he can wait no longer, he can make a calm, controlled exit. As he nears the surface, he should raise his hands above his head to warn the oncoming rescuer and to protect himself.

Side Rescue

In the side rescue, the rescuer places her kayak parallel to the victim's kayak and offers her paddle to help the victim right herself (fig. 5-8A). This paddle forms a bridge across the two kayaks, providing a support that the upturned paddler cannot dislodge or push away during the act of pulling up to the surface (fig. 5-8B). This is by far the safest method of Eskimo rescue. Paddler A's kayak can approach the victim from any direction. The rescuer paddles either backward, forward, or sideways by means of a draw stroke. In some

5-8. The Eskimo side rescue

cases, it might even be more prudent for a rescuer who is approaching for a bow rescue to turn off at the last moment and perform a side rescue instead of risking injury.

It is important that A place her paddle well across the upturned hull. At the same time she places the victim's nearest hand onto the paddle shaft. While she waits for A to place her hands on the shaft, the victim must control her anxiety and refrain from putting a vicelike grip on the first thing that her hand touches. If she grips the part of the paddle shaft on the opposite side to the rescuer, she could foul up the rescue, prolong the time that she has to spend underwater, and cause a distressingly hysterical scene.

The moment B feels her hand placed onto A's paddle shaft, she should pull herself to the surface using both hands. As the kayak turns toward the surface, B may find it necessary to change her hand position.

During the moment of capsize, B may notice that A is parallel to her but is downwind some distance away. This means that the speed of the rescuer's draw stroke will be slow. Paddler B can help things considerably by swimming her kayak toward the rescuer.

Swimming with the Kayak

The ability to swim with a kayak is an excellent survival exercise. If a paddle is lost during a capsize, it can be retrieved without leaving the cockpit. A capsized victim can assist in a practical way during Eskimo rescues by, if necessary, swimming his boat nearer to the rescuing kayak. The methods of swimming vary. Some people prefer to use a dog paddle, others use a kind of breaststroke. I prefer to use the method shown in figure 5-9. The right arm does a crawl stroke, while the other arm performs a powerful dog paddle and never breaks the surface. Some people find it diffi-

5-9. Swimming with the kayak to retrieve a paddle

5-10. Swimming with the paddle

cult to raise their heads high enough to breathe and are, therefore, limited in the distance they can travel. Others appear to have no such problems and can swim indefinitely.

Paddle Swimming

As well as being a good swimming pool exercise, paddle swimming has its survival applications, such as retrieving paddles during rescues. Quite fast speeds can be attained, but the secret is to roll the paddle blade forward on each stroke. The paddle blade is presented flat to the surface of the water and the downward push makes breathing easy by lifting the head out of the water. In figure 5-10, the driving faces are crosshatched and the back of the blade clear.

Factors Affecting Rescues

The success of all the rescues I have illustrated depends very much on a number of factors:

- The age and physical condition of the participants.
- Their level of fear and their general morale.
- The type of personal buoyancy and the clothing they are wearing.
- The distance between the group members at the time of the capsize.
- The skill level of the group and the speed with which they can maneuver.
- The condition of the sea and the strength of the wind.
- The distance from shore and the proximity of rocks.
- The temperature of the water.
- The weight of the equipment inside the upturned boat.
- The amount of equipment carried on the deck and how secure it is.
- The time of day and the presence or absence of fog.

- The prevalence of shipping.
- The amount of buoyancy inside the kayaks.
- The personal qualities and experience of the leader.

If a member of your group capsizes accidentally and the group consists mostly of novices, something has gone wrong with your plans. Either you have bitten off more than they can chew or the weather and tide have changed to the extent that the paddle is no longer a safe proposition, and you should start to think of the quickest and safest way back to sheltered water.

A Last Word on Rescues

It has to be acknowledged that there comes a time when conditions take on a severity that makes any deep-water rescue quite impossible. Even putting oneself close to a swimming kayaker and his boat may place the rescuer in danger of having a person and an upturned kayak planted firmly on his head, followed closely by a dumping deep-water wave. In such a case, the only solution is to send out a distress signal and keep the capsized paddler in sight until help arrives.

SPECIAL PROBLEMS AFLOAT

Repairs Afloat

Kayaks can develop leaks on the open sea from a variety of causes. A collision while paddling too close to others in a following sea is a frequent cause. Sometimes a fault in manufacture can cause the same thing to happen in a less obvious manner. Careless launching is also a cause. I remember

6-1. Repairing a kayak at sea

once paddling 3 miles out at sea in a kayak that I thought had its rear compartment filled with bricks. The explanation was simple: It was full of water. During the launch from a sandy beach, the boat had rested on the upturned base of a broken bottle, producing several holes of varying size.

Whatever the cause of the damage, something must be done immediately. The victim should come alongside the rescuer, but face in the opposite direction. The victim then places his paddle behind his back and across the two boats. In that way he can steady it with both hands while he sits on it and proceeds to change boats. Once the victim is astride the rescuer's boat, the damaged kayak is lifted across the foredeck (fig. 6-1).

Nervous victims may feel safer sitting astride the reardeck so that they can hang onto the person in the rescuing craft. The boat to be repaired, however, forms an outrigger and stabilizes both boats so that it is just as easy for the victim to straddle the foredeck with his kayak between himself and the rescuer (fig. 6-2). In this way the victim can assist with the repair by steadying his kayak and by holding onto the repair kit container.

The leader of the group should make sure that everybody's repair kit is accessible so the person

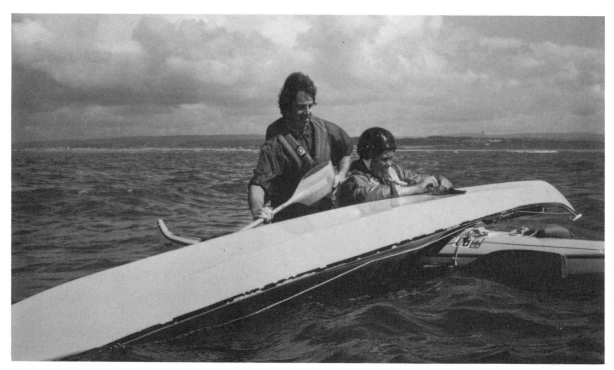

6-2. Assisting with a repair job

doing the repairs can reach into someone else's kayak for a repair kit instead of having to retrieve his own from behind his seat.

If the hole is not too far underneath the hull, it is possible for the occupant of the damaged kayak to lean right over onto one side, supported by someone else, while a third person quickly dries the affected area and sticks a patch on.

Towing

Towing can be hard, grueling work that nobody enjoys, but it is important to have the stamina to be able to tow someone should the need arise—and it usually arises in the worst possible conditions. It could be that one of your companions has been taken ill, is injured, or just overcome by fatigue. Whatever the reason, he is not going to make it back to shore under his own power, so he will have to be towed. To be able to tow him, you must have a towline, of course (see pp. 15–16).

Figure 6-3 shows five towing methods. The method you choose will depend on a number of factors, such as the distance involved, the strength of the rest of the group, the prevailing sea and weather conditions, the type of kayak you are paddling, and how straight the boat you are attempting to tow runs.

If a long haul is anticipated and the group is a strong one, two paddlers towing in tandem will have no difficulty in maintaining the speed of the main party (fig. 6-3A).

Leaders of small groups who are short of help must perform the tow with a single paddler (fig. 6-3B). A long towline is safer than a short one in rough water, especially in following seas.

For paddlers who are nervous and tired or

6-3. Methods for towing an ill or injured paddler

those who might capsize at any moment, the safest way to tow them with limited assistance is to use a towline short enough to allow them to hold onto the stern of the towing kayak (fig. 6-3C). Paddling is difficult for the person towing, however, and the tandem method just described would be far less tiring.

With plenty of help, the easiest way of towing someone who needs constant support is to use two paddlers towing in tandem with a third paddler alongside supporting the person being towed (fig. 6-3D).

The method of getting an unconscious person to safety is illustrated in figure 6-3E. One paddler tows two kayaks across which the victim is laid. The kayakers in the rear hold on tightly to the victim, hold on to each other (to keep their kayaks together so a platform is maintained for the victim), and also hold their paddles in place with their elbows. Mouth-to-mouth resuscitation could be carried out while on the move. Two people towing in tandem will make the tow more efficient.

Although most victims will eventually make it to shore, while they are being towed they immediately run the risk of exposure. They may have been paddling for some time and therefore are wet with perspiration. The sudden inactivity and even a slight breeze will chill them down rapidly. Little can be done about this except to make certain the victim is adequately clothed.

Handling Dangerous Situations

Collision

The problem is not so much a *collision* but rather getting *run down* by someone else. There is a difference. Kayaks sit low in the water, so even in good visibility and calm weather, it is easy for them to go unnoticed in busy shipping lanes. As inland and coastal waterways become more congested, the risk of being run down increases. As far as recreational small boats are concerned, many collisions are alcohol related. Things are now so bad that it has been suggested in some areas that small boat users face alcohol tests like any car driver. In recent years, boats on the U.S. Intracoastal Waterway have been especially prone to this type of accident.

To minimize your risk for a collision, take the following precautions:

1. Use highly visible equipment. Use day glow colors for your life-jacket, clothing, deck equipment and at least one face of your paddle blades.

2. Know where you are in relation to the shipping fairway, any channel markers, and other water users.

3. Try to spot trouble a long way off. If traffic is busy and fast moving, try to keep to less traveled areas, such as areas out of the shipping lanes or shallower waters.

4. In fog or bad visibility, consider using a small radar reflector. Carry a small, hand-held fog

horn. If you think a collision likely sound five blasts.

5. If you cross a shipping lane, do so as a group. Do not pass in front of other boat users as a long strung-out line.

6. If a small boat is bearing down on you at high speed and you think that you have not been seen, extend your paddle vertically into the air and wave it slowly back and forth. The bright side of the blade should be pointed toward the oncoming craft.

7. At night carry more than the mandatory white light. Provide yourself with a powerful hand-held beam or headlight. You can then direct it at any craft that may be approaching in a threatening manner. Do not, of course, blind the helmsman.

Moored Vessels

Kayaks are ideal craft for exploring harbors, estuaries, and busy rivers—but beware of the dangers. One of the rules is to keep away from the upstream end of moored vessels. Large ships are often berthed side by side and are separated only by buffers that leave a small gap of about one foot at the narrowest point. Anyone swept into this position is in great danger (see fig. 6-4).

To prevent himself from being swept into the narrowest position between the ships and either crushed by them or sucked underneath them and drowned, a victim must use his paddle, elbows, or arms to wedge himself against the ships (fig. 6-4A). If the victim is alone, he stands little chance of surviving unless he can attract attention by shouting.

If the victim is accompanied by only one other kayaker, the other person must immediately go for help. This person may have to moor his boat and climb to the top of a quay to alert the ships involved so that a rope can be dropped down to the trapped paddler. (There are usually plenty of ladders leading up from the water level, though many of these are dilapidated and dangerous [fig. 6-4B].)

6-4. This shows a rescue attempt of a kayaker trapped between two moored vessels.

If a group of kayakers is involved, a rescue can meanwhile be attempted by the leader or someone he designates. The rest of the group must hold position against the tidal flow well away from the danger area (fig. 6-4C). The rescuer should paddle toward the victim (fig. 6-4D) and throw a line in to him. If a line cannot be thrown to the victim, it can be attached to a life jacket or buoyancy aid and floated to him. If possible, the victim should secure the line to his own deck line and allow it to run along the deck line toward the bow of his kayak as he is pulled out.

The rescuer's towline must have some means of quick release to be used should he also find himself in danger of being drawn between the vessels.

Fallen Trees

Although danger from fallen trees normally occurs on rapid rivers, similar difficulties can arise on tidal waters between closely packed islands. A kayaker who is careless or unaware of the dangers could find himself in the predicament depicted in figure 6-5. Not only is this a dangerous situation, it could be fatal. Just how bad things really are depends on the strength of the victim and the kind of grip he has on the tree, the force of the water pressing against him, how much of the tree is underneath the water, and the time it takes for help to arrive. The illustration shows rapidly moving water flowing against an old, fallen tree; however, the water does not have to be flowing fast, nor the tree dead. A highly respected kayak coach once referred to a weeping willow with green branches resting gently on the surface of a slow-moving river as "whispering death"—how right he was!

Action must be taken quickly, with these questions in mind:

- Can someone land on the bank without any great loss of valuable time?
- Is it possible for rescuers to climb along the tree?
- Is the victim in or out of his kayak?
- If the victim is with a group of kayakers, the other kayakers can simultaneously attempt a rescue. One person can land, climb along the tree, and secure a holding rope around the victim. It may be necessary to fasten two ropes to the victim (see fig. 6-6), one to hold him in place and the other to be taken upstream from the tree so that his body can be pulled out and away from the tree that the water is forcing him against.
- If the victim is still in the kayak, he may be held prisoner in the cockpit by water pressure, and it may be necessary to puncture the hull of the boat to release this pressure and the victim. If the rescuer is not carrying a strong diving knife or an ax, this can prove an almost impossible task.

In figure 6-5 the rescuer, B, has paddled into a position upstream where he is in no danger. The rescuer throws or floats a flotation device (for example, a life jacket) attached to a towline to the victim, A. Unless the rescuer is very strong, it is almost impossible for him to tow the victim off the tree. It is better if a line is taken ashore and passed to someone who has a footing firm enough to ensure that the pull is a positive one. It also might be possible to float a line down to the victim from the bank, but this will depend on the nature of the bank and how quickly a landing can be made.

Speed is vital. It takes only a minute or so for the victim to panic or tire and release his grip—

6-5. A kayaker trapped against a fallen tree awaits rescue by rope and flotation device.

6-6. When a kayaker is trapped against a fallen tree, it may be necessary to secure the victim with one rope while pulling him away with another.

assuming that he has been able to get a firm grip in the first place.

Any kayaker in danger of being trapped against a tree should throw his body over the trunk or nearest stout branch. He should twist his body so that the bottom of the hull of the kayak faces upstream. He should do everything possible to prevent the cockpit from turning to face upstream; if that should happen, he could become trapped and his life would be in imminent danger. Once the underside of the hull is facing upstream, he should release the spray cover and pull himself onto the tree. He must disregard the fate of the kayak until he is safely out of it.

To release a kayak that is trapped against a tree, the cockpit must be turned so that it faces downstream. In this way the water should drain out. It may be possible at this stage to lift the kayak out of the water. If not, a rope should be attached to the toggle nearest the bank, and the boat should be pulled to shore.

Mud Flats and Quicksand

Kayakers must be especially careful when exploring very flat country in areas of heavy rainfall. These areas can be filled with bogs and

quicksand. Likewise, when the tide drains from large flat estuaries and inlets, it can leave many miles of soft sand or leg-sucking mud. In some places the mud and sand may be deep and highly dangerous. Under no circumstances should a paddler leave his kayak. It will provide support in many conditions.

If faced with a large expanse of mud of unknown depth and consistency, a kayaker should either be patient and wait until the tide turns and floats him off or drag the kayak behind him, testing the surface in front with the paddle.

A kayaker who does find himself waist deep in mud should first pull the kayak to him and use it for support. If it is obvious that the mud is too deep to walk across safely, he should sit astride the boat and slide it forward over the mud, making sure to stop moving it while there is still plenty of buoyant hull underneath. Next he must extricate his legs and hitch forward along the kayak before sliding the boat forward again. This can be slow, but a person in this situation will be quite safe so long as there is always some part of the kayak underneath him.

Remember at all times, keep calm, keep together, and keep the kayaks with you.

A person who is wandering the shore alone without his kayak and finds himself sinking into mud or sand should lie across the surface and attempt to move forward by "swimming" with a breaststroke.

Floating Ice

Paddling near large lumps of ice or small icebergs is exciting and very pretty, but a person can become so engrossed that he is not aware of the dangers. Anyone who paddles close to a small iceberg may notice that at water level, the action of the warmer water near the surface undercuts it. The difference in temperature between the water and the ice also acts upon the submerged part of the iceberg. Gradually this will reduce it enough so that it may fracture underwater. This breaking off of ice is called calving.

As is well known, nine-tenths of an iceberg lies under the water. Calving throws this large volume of floating ice off-balance. It then takes up an entirely different angle in the water or rolls over completely—spectacular to watch, but dangerous to be near.

If iceberg A in figure 6-8 calved at fracture point B, the kayakers could be killed by the new iceberg C. New icebergs have sharp, jagged profiles, which indicate that they have never rolled and should be treated with caution. Iceberg D is smooth and round. It has probably rolled at least once already and is much safer to approach.

Whether an iceberg has calved recently is usually indicated by the amount it has been undercut. The deeper the undercut level with the surface, the longer it has been in the same position, and the more likely it will become unbalanced.

Kayakers should beware of extensive areas of floating ice. Although it may appear that there is plenty of paddle room between the pieces, any change of wind or tide could bring it all grinding and crushing together. If the ice is pack ice and therefore flat-topped, it might be possible to climb up onto the floating pieces. Progress can then be made by dragging the kayak along, jumping across the small gaps and paddling across the larger ones. When it comes time to launch again, a side drop may be necessary (see fig. 3-3, p. 35). Glacial ice, however, is almost impossible to climb onto safely, due to its irregular shape and instability.

In some parts of the Arctic, ice along the shore can cause special problems. In figure 6-7 the paddlers are following a "shore lead," a gap between the floating ice and the shore. Although land is only a few yards away, an ice shelf that may run for many miles along a sandless, rocky shore makes it almost inaccessible.

The overhanging wall of hard blue ice is all that is left of sea pack ice, which, at some time, was attached to the shore. With an onshore wind,

High water

Low water

6-7. Kayakers following a shore lead look for a cutting in the ice shaft that will allow them to carry their boats ashore.

6-8. An iceberg ready to calve

the kayakers in the illustration are at great risk, especially with a flooding tide. Landing is possible only where a small rivulet has cut through the ice toward the sea to form a cutting, up which kayaks and equipment can be carried to safety.

Lightning

If you really want to give yourself a scare, try paddling in the middle of a violent thunderstorm. I remember one notable occasion as I sat in my kayak and the rain poured down. The sky was a ghastly, dark grey-green colour and every so often there was a flash of lightning followed by the roar of thunder. The rain fell so hard that every drop jumped back 6 inches into the air as it hit the water. Eventually it was so heavy it seemed to merge with the sky. I remember this storm well, because one bolt of lightning struck the lightning rod on the nearby lighthouse.

To some extent, I was comforted by the fact that I had read somewhere that the odds against getting struck by lightening are millions and mil-

lions to one. The trouble was that the writer of this profundity had gone on to say that if you were alone and you were the highest point in the middle of an open space—and you were in the middle of a thunderstorm—the odds were then diminished to the degree that if a lottery prize were offered at the same odds, there would be a rush to buy tickets. Like the vast majority of people who are forced to suffer thunderstorms out in the open, however, I survived to tell the tale.

Let us identify the enemy. Inside thunder clouds, tiny droplets of moisture combine with the flow of the air mass to create electrical charges. The electrical differences between the ground, in this case the surface of the sea, or between one pocket of air and another, build up until what is known as a small "leader" stroke clears an electrical pathway for a massive "return" stroke. It is this hundred-million–volt release of energy that we see as the spectacular flash of lightning. When you are alone and feeling vulnerable on a wide expanse of open water, you will be comforted to know that five out of six of these flashes happen high up in the clouds and never reach the earth.

The main trouble occurs when the lightning uses your body to find its way to "ground" (in our case the sea). Where lightning will strike is anybody's guess. It has been known to select one person in a tightly packed crowd and hurt no one else, yet in 1918 one flash killed a complete flock of more than 500 sheep.

In some ways lightning is predictable. It needs to find the easiest path on its way to "earth" and will try to find the highest point. In the fraction of a second it takes to strike, it has been known to travel down through wet clothing and burn its way out through the soles of people's shoes. Some people have even been struck more than once.

Never seek shelter under a tree. Normally, the lightning will choose to run down the moist layer underneath the bark. If you are standing under the tree, you become the easiest way for the lightning to reach the ground so the lightning will then choose *your* tree. If you are under cover, stand well back. If you are standing in the mouth of a cave watching the storm, the lightning can jump the short distance between the roof of the cave and your head and use your body on its path to "earth."

Whether or not you live or die will depend on the route the lightning takes past your vital organs. The worst that can happen is that the bolt will hit the top of your head and pass through your heart.

Now let us look on the bright side. Scores of people who are struck by lightning every year are knocked unconscious and suffer only from shock. Unlike the situation with an ordinary electric shock, the heart of a lightning victim can be started again with a normal rhythm by the timely application of artificial resuscitation. In other words, if you are holding a paddle that is a good conductor, the chances are that the shock will pass down the paddle, only knocking you unconscious and therefore knocking you into the water as it does so. If you are unwise enough to be paddling alone, you should ensure that you are wearing some kind of buoyancy aid or a PFD that will float your body in the head-out-of-the-water survival position. If you are not alone, your partners should waste no time in grabbing you by the hair and clearing your head from the water. They should then drag you across their decks and give you resuscitation. (See page 128.)

More than a hundred years ago it was discovered that electrostatic charges always collect on the outside of hollow objects—that's why you are safe in your car. Because your kayak is a hollow object, any charge will travel around your hull—the only snag is that you are sticking out of the hole in the top and the lightning is going to use you on its journey down to the wet hull.

If I lived in an area where violent thunderstorms were the norm and I wanted to get some excitement by going out in the storms, I would

6-9. A properly grounded conductor should theoretically give you an imaginary cone of protection formed by a 45-to-60-degree angle from the top of your rod.

Rod extends above head or paddle height.

Battery jump lead cable with clamp.

Plastic or Fibreglass Saddle fastened to rear deck.

To ground (water)

6-10. A homemade saddle could be moulded from fiberglass and fastened behind the paddler by the rear deck elastics.

consider fixing a lightning conductor to my kayak (see fig. 6-9). I would find a piece of thin metal rod made of material that is a good conductor. (Copper is best but a couple of spring-jointed tent poles should also work.) I would then secure the rod into a socket held in position by some kind of saddle (fig. 6-10), which in turn would be held in place by some elastics on the rear deck. It would have to be in reach of my hand and the rod would have to be higher than my head—I suppose it should really be higher than my paddle when in its highest position. I would then be able to erect my conductor or dismantle it at will and stow it away when out at sea. In theory any lightning strike would find the conductor and be guided down to "earth" via the hull. A proper lightning conductor should protect you and your kayak under an imaginary cone formed by a 45-to-60-degree angle extending from the top of the rod.

After all these precautions are taken, there are still those who feel that a conductor just invites a lightning strike for the very good reason that you are giving the lightning an easy path to ground. One fact I am sure of—I will never be frightened by the thunder of the lightning strike that proves me wrong.

HANDLING DOUBLE KAYAKS

Double Kayaks

Because double kayaks can be sailed or slept in, long-distance journeys are not governed by the paddlers' waking hours. Meals can be taken or even cooked on the move. With lee boards down and mast up, it is possible to forget about paddling and sail a double quite successfully over quite long distances. Proof of all these points lies in the fact that double kayaks have crossed the Atlantic Ocean three times.

Because of its width, a double is sympathetic to slow responses and poor technique. Unfortunately, this means that after their introduction to the sport many double paddlers remain quite satisfied with a technical repertoire that consists of nothing more adventurous than a forward paddling stroke.

In certain areas and in sheltered conditions, doubles can be a good way of introducing people to the delights of the open sea. If an instructor occupies the rearmost position, a student can be under observation at all times.

Double kayaks used on the open sea should exhibit certain qualities. Widths should be 30 to 36 inches and lengths 19 to 22 feet. Short doubles of

wide beam handle like slugs and should be avoided unless they are to be used as play boats. Deep-sea doubles should have enough volume to carry two people and all the equipment necessary for a prolonged trip in a wilderness area.

Cockpits or seating positions should separate clumsy and uncoordinated paddlers from their partners. This will prevent paddlers from clacking together and will preserve harmony.

When paddling, or in the event of a capsize, seats and thigh supports should be fixed firmly in position. For long-distance expedition work, however, it should be possible to remove them so that one or both occupants can wriggle down in the cockpits and shelter inside the hull.

From an economical point of view, a double kayak will cost less to buy than two single boats. But although it should paddle faster than a single, it will not paddle twice as fast, nor will it carry twice the equipment.

On your journeys you will never be short of company, but this can be a mixed blessing. Harmony comes with practice, and if it does not exist between the pair on land, it is not going to materialize on the water.

In rough conditions or in a capsize situation, it

is worth remembering that all your eggs are in one basket. Because of this, all the deep-water rescues applicable to double kayaks should be practiced in controlled conditions and well in advance of a trip.

Fiberglass Double Kayaks

The Eddyline designed by Werner Furrer, the Sisiutle designed by Lee Moyer, and the Seascape designed by John Abbenhouse (fig. 7-1) are the only double kayaks I am familiar with that are available in both North America and the United Kingdom and that I would consider to be well-designed boats.

The Sisiutle can be purchased with three cockpits, but with this added facility paddling space is very limited. I think the center cockpit is best reserved for rescue purposes or for some small nonpaddling passenger. If the Sisiutle is to be used on rough water, I would suggest that the seats be secured more firmly to the hull of the boat. For those who like steeply angled decks, those on the Sisiutle have excellent water-shedding properties.

The Eddyline is an extremely comfortable kayak to paddle and is a very seaworthy craft. I have also seen it carry a sail to good advantage. I consider its molded bucket seats much more practical than the loose-fitting variety.

The Seascape is a newcomer to the doubles scene and is a welcome addition. It has a powerful, seaworthy bow that rises well to choppy seas, and the large volume hull makes it possible for the occupants to be self-sufficient for long periods. In its appearance and seaworthiness, the Seascape resembles the ancient two-manhole baidarkas more than any other double kayak that I have seen on the market.

The Aleut Sea II, designed in 1986 by Howard Jeffs, was one of the forerunners of what can only be described as a new breed of double touring kayak. The boat has a length of twenty-two feet and a width of twenty-six inches. These dimen-

7-1. Nonfolding double kayak

7-2. Modern replica of a two-manhole baidarka

sions give it a huge volume for storage, while the length enables the paddlers to maintain a high average speed. The cockpits are far enough apart to allow each occupant to paddle at his own speed and not necessarily in time with his partner.

The boat in figure 7-2 has five watertight bulkheads. There is one in front of the front footrest, one behind the front seat, and one in front of the rear footrest. Immediately behind the rear seat are two bulkheads about a foot apart. This small, secondary compartment has a round hatch and holds any small items that might be needed by the rear paddler while on the water. Although the front paddler can also have a small, behind-the-back storage compartment, the kayak from which figure 7-2 was drawn had its center compartment converted to carry two small children—hence the very large cover over the seating space in the middle of the boat.

The kayak used as the model for this illustration has an added feature. Behind each cockpit and secured to the deck is a small pouch, sealed by Velcro. Each pouch contains a rope stirrup to assist paddlers in heaving their bodies from the water during deep-water reentries. The business of emptying and then reentering a capsized, swamped, and unaccompanied double kayak has presented problems in the past. The addition of watertight compartments has helped ease these difficulties.

The Aleut Sea II is fitted with a foredeck hand-operated pump. The pump's detachable handle can be seen housed in its own recess to the left and in front of the foremost cockpit. Recessed lifting handles are positioned on either side of the center opening. Any kayak that is 22 feet long is not easily carried on your car roof. This particular double can be built in two manageable sections that are joined at the bulkheads.

It is perhaps worth noting that since my own small group crossed the North Sea in single kayaks in 1976, the only other paddlers to make the same west–east crossing were Kevin Danforth and Franco Ferraro in an Aleut Sea II in May 1989.

7-3. An Aleut Sea II is poised on the crest of a wave in the Gulf of Corryvrecken. These waves form part of the Great Race close to the infamous whirlpool. When conditions are rough, taking photos from a solo kayak is always a little nerve wracking. A double kayak, on the other hand, gives the photographer more security and therefore more time. Unfortunately the approaching wave shown in the picture almost back looped the double kayak from which this photo was taken. (Photo courtesy Barry Howell)

Folding Double Kayaks

There are a number of folding kayaks on the market, and the two most popular designs are made in Europe. The Klepper, made in Germany, is an old favorite. It is carried in two bags, and when assembled it makes a double kayak 17 feet long by 35 inches wide. The one-man version is 15 feet long by 28 inches wide. The frames are of mountain ash joined by fittings of aluminum. The whole affair is covered with a skin of Hypalon and canvas. Air-filled sponsons are incorporated into the cover, which will float the kayak in the event of a capsize. The Klepper has a considerable freeboard, and this could prove difficult in high winds.

The Nautiraid, made in France, is a beautifully built kayak with a slightly lower freeboard than the Klepper. It, too, has sponsons as part of its integral design, but these do not influence the tension of the cover as they do in the Klepper. The double version contains fourteen pieces, which can be put together in just over a quarter of an hour. The completed double is 16 feet, 6 inches long by 36 inches wide, but the kayak is designed so that it can be used by a single paddler. The

Nautiraid single is short by seagoing standards—only 13 feet, 6 inches long by 36 inches wide. Like the Klepper, however, it comes equipped with a rudder that compensates for any tendency to yaw.

The most revolutionary folding design I have ever seen is the Feathercraft, which comes from Canada. It is the brainchild of Doug Simpson of Vancouver, who has abandoned traditional materials like wood and canvas in favor of more modern substances. The result is a folding kayak that is lighter, quicker, easier to assemble, and easier to care for. The frame consists of high-tensile aluminum tubing. The longitudinal members are shock corded like tent poles for easy assembly. These attach to a welded cockpit. Once the frame is together and the cover is in place, the stern deck bar is hinged and becomes the tool used to expand the frame lengthwise, thus tensioning the skin. The hull material consists of a layer of Butyl rubber sandwiched between two layers of woven nylon. The deck is made of waterproofed nylon pack cloth, and the spray cover is sewn directly onto the deck to become a part of it. Like other folding kayaks the Feathercraft has air sponsons built into the gunwales.

The Feathercraft comes in a single as well as a double version. The single is a sensible 14 feet, 8 inches long and 26 inches wide and weighs a mere 38 pounds. The double is 18 feet long by 32 inches wide and weighs 50 pounds. The Feathercraft is portable. The frame breaks down to form a backpack that includes shoulder straps and a hip belt.

Paddles

Doubles have wider, fuller hulls than single boats, and because of this I prefer to use a paddle at least a foot longer than the one I would normally use in a single. Some paddlers like them even

7-4. Sometimes the Inuit had to find space for the family without the advantage of two cockpits. Is that a small face we see peeping out above the front of the cockpit coaming?

longer, and this is especially preferable if a rudder is not being used.

Packing

Because a double is by necessity a roomy craft, it can beget or encourage disorganized packing. I am a great believer in dividing a kayak into watertight compartments with watertight access hatches and some kind of bailing pump as part of the everyday equipment. This gives the occupants the responsibility of considering the order and method of storage.

Safety

Naturally, all safety considerations that apply to single craft apply to the double. Boats should be equipped with taut deck lines, paddle parks, chart and compass, elastics and towlines, flares, and first-aid and repair kits for both day trips and long-distance journeys.

Technique

The techniques required of the double kayaker are basically the same as those of the paddler of single craft. However, the two paddlers often perform different strokes at the same time and, done properly, in synchronization.

Ideally paddling should be done in unison, but with inexperienced partners this can be more a dream than a reality. It is important that each paddler understands the role of the other. Close to shore or when dodging rocks, the person at the front is the pilot, and it is he who keeps the "captain" or stern paddler informed as to what is going on up ahead. It is the job of the stern paddler to steer and direct the boat, while the bow paddler keeps the kayak moving through the water at a steady speed by maintaining his forward stroke. So that teamwork can develop between partners, pairs should paddle together over varying distances, and under diverse sea conditions.

Although any change of direction should be done by the stern paddler in doubles kayaking, track deviation is probably best corrected by using a rudder. This eliminates the necessity of leaning the boat over onto one side—a more difficult maneuver with two paddlers than with one.

Launching

A double kayak can be launched in the same manner as a single kayak. Less strain will be placed on the hull, however, if the bow paddler is settled into position first while the fore-end of the boat is supported by the water.

If the beach slopes steeply and the water is calm, the kayak can be placed parallel to the shore

and the paddles used for support while you enter the boat.

Forward Paddling

Once partners acquire a little harmony and develop an easy, relaxed forward paddle stroke, daily cruising distance should be equal to, if not better than a single kayak's 10 to 15 miles on an easy day or 20 to 25 miles with a little effort.

Turning and Maneuvering

The stern paddler can make small changes in direction or corrections of track by applying ruddering strokes when necessary. If more help is needed, the bow paddler can assist by paddling slightly harder on the opposite side from which you wish to turn. In this manner, corrections are done without any loss of forward speed.

Turning through 360 Degrees

Turning through 360 degrees requires the sweep and reverse sweep strokes, which are performed by both paddlers in unison. The bow paddler sweeps out on the side opposite to which the turn is to be made. At the same time, the stern paddler executes a reverse sweep on the side opposite to the bow paddler's stroke (fig. 7-5A). If the strokes are done with equal force and simultaneously, the kayak will pivot around easily in a graceful turn (fig. 7-5B). A normal draw stroke, performed simultaneously on opposite sides by both paddlers, will turn a stationary double.

Fast Turn

As the name implies, the fast turn, or low telemark (fig. 7-6), can be done successfully only

7-5. The reverse and sweep strokes, performed simultaneously on opposite sides, will turn a double kayak through 360 degrees.

7-7. To move diagonally sideways, the stern paddler performs a reverse sweep on one side, while the bow paddler performs a bow rudder on the opposite side.

7-6. The fast turn or low telemark

when the kayak is moving forward fast—the faster the better. On a prearranged signal, the paddlers stop their forward stroke and place their paddle blades out into the water with their leading edges high. The paddles will plane on the surface of the water and will be in a position to support both the paddlers, who now lean over into the turn putting the gunwale underwater. The kayak will turn quickly and in a spectacular manner. As the forward speed decreases, however, both paddlers must sweep their paddles forward, so that they finish sitting in an upright position.

Reverse Sweep and Bow Rudder

As the kayak moves forward, the stern paddler performs a reverse sweep on one side while the bow paddler executes what is called a bow rudder—the paddle is placed well out from the side with the driving face of the blade facing in toward the bow. The bow paddler's thumbs point upward (fig. 7-7). The reverse sweep and bow rudder complement each other, and the kayak moves diagonally sideways in the direction of the paddle. If the bow paddler inadvertently draws the driving face of her paddle inward, instead of holding it steady, the stroke then becomes a bow draw. This is not really what you want to do because the bow draw is a very strong stroke, strong enough to halt the diagonal movement of the kayak and turn the kayak's bow in the direction of the paddle. Practice on the part of the bow paddler will result in a good, nonretarding bow rudder.

7-8. The draw stroke

Draw Stroke

Doubles can be moved sideways in exactly the same way as a single kayak, using the draw stroke (fig. 7-8). As with all other double strokes, it is important that both paddlers stroke together. Otherwise the kayak will turn instead of moving sideways.

A good draw stroke may be necessary when positioning for a rescue or when caving, dodging rocks, or just coming alongside.

Deep-Water Rescues

Anyone can capsize. You may feel stable and secure in your nice, wide double kayak when most of your paddling is done on fairly flat water, and because of this a capsize will be all the more disturbing when it comes. I would advise pairs who paddle together regularly to practice their emergency drills in calm, warm water before paddling off into the open sea. Make sure you keep your paddles under control. If you have done your packing correctly, you should not see any of your equipment floating out of the cockpit. For added

stability, the paddle float can be used with any of the rescues and reentries described below.

Rescue of an Unescorted Double Kayak

The kayak first must be turned the right way up, with as little water as possible allowed to collect inside. To do this the two paddlers should position themselves on the same downwind side of the boat and near the center. At a signal, they both lift and flip the kayak over and away from themselves, thus scooping up as little water as possible into the cockpit.

The stern paddler should enter first so that he can watch and steady the kayak while reentry is made into the forward cockpit. There are two ways of doing this. As one paddler holds the bow tightly, the other pulls himself up onto the reardeck and hitches along toward the nearest cockpit (fig. 7-9). This method can be tricky in rough conditions. A second and more positive method is for the bow paddler to steady the kayak by hanging on to one side of the stern cockpit while the stern paddler climbs in from the other side (fig. 7-10A). The stern paddler then sculls for support while his partner reenters (fig. 7-10B).

Once both paddlers are back in position, it is worth remembering that they are now facing the conditions that capsized them in the first place. Because of this, one paddler must maintain the support strokes while the other gets to work and attempts to bail the boat dry.

It is possible for each paddler to have his own bailer and to pump the kayak out together. The

7-9. One method of reentering the kayak after a capsize

7-10. An effective method of reentry is for the stern paddler to enter first (A) and then scull for support while the bow paddler reenters (B).

paddles are supported across the shoulders, and the occupants scull together on opposite sides. In this way the boat will be emptied in half the time.

H Deep-Water Rescue of an Escorted Kayak

For some years now, the H rescue has not been used by paddlers of single kayaks as a method of emptying an upturned boat. This is

7-11. The H rescue is a method of emptying a double kayak.

because the occupants of the rescuing boats, who had to heave up and down on a kayak half-full of water, had difficulty staying upright. Holding the boats parallel was an additional problem. With doubles, these problems do not exist, and the H rescue (fig. 7-11) is an ideal way of emptying any escorted double that is not intolerably weighted down with expedition equipment. Any tendency on the part of the rescue craft to swing around can be corrected by the paddler not involved in the lifting. If the water is very cold, the paddlers can sit on the decks of the rescuing craft and assist by sculling for support on one side. The methods of reentry are similar to those used for solo craft. The easiest method is for a double to pull alongside an already righted craft so the two seated paddlers can hold onto the empty cockpits and steady the boat for the two swimming paddlers to reenter, one at a time.

SAILING YOUR KAYAK

To a kayaker the wind need not be seen as an enemy. With good, reasonably priced sailing rig— or with a parafoil kite—you will soon discover that the wind can be a very good companion. Sailing a kayak can give you a serene, effortless journey or a thrill-a-minute ride. It all depends on the size of your sail, the strength of the wind, *and how good a sailor you are.*

Until a few years ago, this part of our paddle sport was greatly neglected. A few long-distance journeys across the open sea and along wilderness coastlines drew attention to the fact that kayaks could be sailed with great efficiency, but few paddlers actually took the trouble to give it a try. Sailing kayaks built for touring first developed a following on Scotland's west coast in the 1920s and 1930s. In boats made from lath and canvas, kayakers would paddle out from the mainland with sails furled and cruise among the maze of islands that make up the Inner and Outer Hebrides. They would then enjoy an effortless trip back to the mainland under full sail, taking advantage of the prevailing westerly winds. For most kayakers today, a sail is still merely a supplement to the paddle, but there are an ever-increasing number of enthusiasts who are choosing sailpower as their sole means of propulsion.

Most single kayaks will take a sail, but double kayaks—because of their width and roominess— are especially suited to sailing. A solo paddler in a double kayak will have "cabin space." Certainly there should be enough room to bed down and sleep. Any double kayak fitted with a sail of suitable size will slide smoothly over the surface of the sea, and even the beamiest, heaviest boat will require very little sail area to turn it into a virtual flying machine. If you intend to do a fair amount of sailing, you will find a rudder especially useful.

Masts and Sails

If you aim to take up kayak sailing seriously, or even if you only wish to experiment, you will soon discover that there is a wide assortment of sailing rigs from which to choose. You will probably not end up with the first sailing rig that you try. Paddlers tend to change their rig as they become more competent. The secret is not to be too ambitious at first.

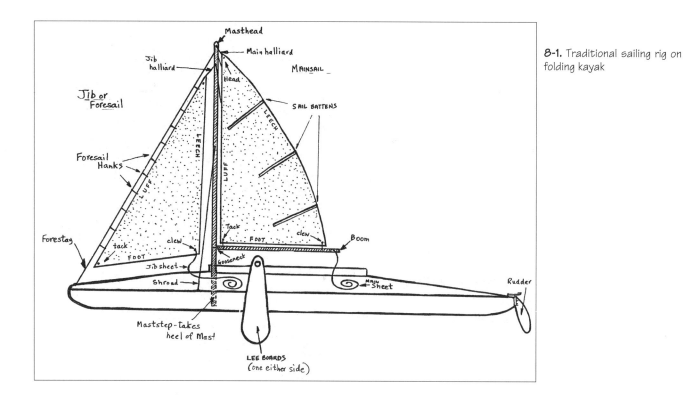

Masthead
Main halliard
Jib halliard
Head
MAINSAIL
Jib or Foresail
SAIL BATTENS
LEECH
Foresail Hanks
LUFF
LEECH
LUFF
Tack
Forestay
clew
FOOT
clew
Boom
tack
FOOT
Gooseneck
Jib sheet
MAIN Sheet
Shroad
Rudder
Maststep-takes heel of Mast
LEE BOARDS
(one either side)

8-1. Traditional sailing rig on folding kayak

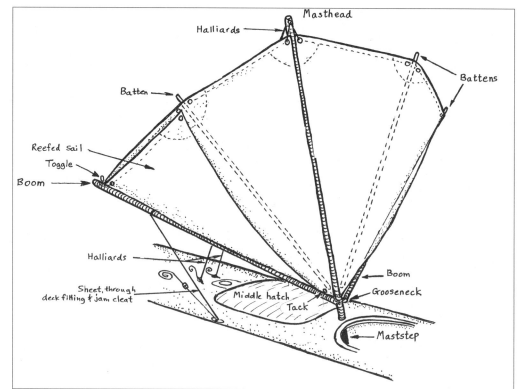

Masthead
Halliards
Battens
Batten
Reefed sail
Toggle
Boom
Boom
Gooseneck
Halliards
Middle hatch
Tack
Sheet, through deck fitting & jam cleat
Maststep

8-2. Key to fan sail

The first item of equipment you'll need is something upon which to hang the sail. Masts can be single stem or A poles, and you can carry one or two depending on the amount of sail you want. Some boats have ready-made mast sockets. There are also conversion kits available. If you happen to be handy with plywood and fiberglass, you can design your own mast-step or socket. A serviceable mast can be made from a telescopic boat hook.

Sails come in two basic shapes—square and triangular—and in various sizes. One variation is the fan-shaped sail. These are supported by two poles fixed in the shape of a V, the apex of which points toward the deck. The paddler controls this type of rig by means of two hand-held lines, known as "sheets," which can be tied off, allowing one to brace or supplement the wind by paddling. Square sails are also favored by some; these allow you to paddle and sail at the same time. As with the fan shape, however, when using a square sail you are limited to "running" with the wind. You will be unable to sail on a "reach," that is, at right angles across the wind. If you want to turn your kayak into a real sailboat, there are a number of conventional sailing rigs on the market, but you will have to make some other modifications.

Outriggers, Daggerboards, and Leeboards

Unless you take precautions, the larger the area of your sail, the greater your chances are of an unplanned swim. To prevent this mishap, you should have some kind of an outrigger if your sail area is more than 24 square feet. The simplest outrigger consists of your paddle stuck out in a low brace position, but this is not much good if you need both hands for managing the boat.

A better solution is to make or buy some kind of securely fixed, rigid outrigger. There now are some excellent systems on the market. You will have to decide whether you want a solid, stream-line outrigger or the type that inflates and can be stowed away together with its supporting poles.

To prevent your kayak from sliding sideways and to complete your conversion, you will also need some kind of daggerboard. This is merely a large skeg or fin, fixed to hang down under the kayak somewhere near the center of the boat. A daggerboard will enable you to sail on a reach or to "beat," that is, to sail at an angle *into* the wind. As with a sailboat, you will be able to "tack," or go into the wind by zig-zagging.

Many of the folding kayaks are intended to be sailed and are therefore supplied with the mounting for a mast. They also have provision for the fitting of two leeboards, one on either side of the boat, which serve the same purpose as the single daggerboard. Usually made of plywood, leeboards are secured to either end of a portable wooden cross thwart. They can also be incorporated into the supporting arms that hold the outriggers.

Do not get complacent just because you now feel you have joined the yachting fraternity. The water is as cold as it ever was, so dress appropriately and continue to wear your PFD at all times. Carry some kind of pump. Performing a deep-water rescue and then emptying the kayak by one of the standard methods will be almost impossible when you have to cope with the added interference of mast, lines, soggy sail, and the outrigger you affixed knowing that it would never have to be unfastened. The good news is that once the boat is the right way up, the outrigger may make your reentry easier.

Build Your Own Sailing Rig

To awaken a do-it-yourself frenzy in my readers, I have included this very successful system, which has been fitted to an Aleut Sea II by Didier (Didi) Plouhinec of Cherbourg, France. His rig was inspired by George Dyson; although the mast is different, the sail is the same size. What follows is Didi's own description.

8-3. An Aleut Sea II with fan-shaped sail is fully rigged and in position. (Photo courtesy Didier Plouhinec)

Mast and Booms

My mast step. This is a piece of windsurf board mast bonded through the deck. The mast step is 30 centimeters long and is situated just behind the front cockpit. It touches the bulkhead and the bottom of the central hatch.

The mast. This is homemade of Oregon pine and Scandinavian fir. Its size is 1.67 meters—1.37 meters above the deck—and the diameter is 38 millimeters. There is no masthead block, just a big hole.

The booms. There are two booms in fir, also homemade. Each is 1.32 meters long and 20 millimeters in diameter and gives a sail opening of 2.68 meters downwind. The gooseneck is a simple rope passed through the mast and tied firmly to the booms. The two "gooseneck lines" are then tied by a reef knot. This is a permanent fastening.

Toggles are fitted to the booms to fasten the sheets and clews. Mast and boom are protected by marine varnish. The lower part of the mast is painted with a mix of marine glue (PPU 100 International) and thinner. This prevents the wood fibers from expanding with moisture.

The Sail

The fan-shape sail of 2.20 square meters is in

8-4. This kayak shows the deck arrangement of lines. (Photo courtesy Didier Plouhinec)

fact two small sails crafted by a professional sail-maker:

- The sizes are 1.25 meters, 1.25 meters, 0.55 meter for the lower panels and 0.66 meter for the upper.
- The canvas is sail nylon.
- On each sail there are two battens in batten pockets. Cavitation can be had in the sails by adjusting small strings.
- On each side of the batten pockets there is an eyelet. The upper one is a reef point, the other a clew. A small toggle on the lowest clew allows the sail to reef.
- A loop (sewn, whipped, and protected as

usual) is passed in the tack.
- The halyard is also sewn and whipped to the head of the sail.

The Lines

The lines are:
- Two halyards, which also serve as backstays. They are 3.20 meters long, although 5 centimeters longer might be better.
- Two sheets of 1.75 meters. These are fastened on the toggle of the boom, 1 meter from the mast.
- These lines are 5 millimeter, cotton covered. They hold in jamcleats better than nylon.
- Two boom vang lines were added in May 1993. Those lines pass through the free holes of the recessed deck fittings.

The Deck

The deck requires:
- Two figure-eight cleats for the halyards, situated on either side of the compass. A hole between the two bolts makes a good fairlead.
- Two fairlead cleats (jamcleats) for the sheets, bolted close to the cleats.
- The chart elastics, which are also practical to keep the lines coiled.
- Two tubular jamcleats for the boom vang lines.

How to Put It All Together

- Fasten the boom to the clew with the toggle.
- Pass the tack loops under the mast and put the mast in its step.
- Fasten the boom gooseneck lines around the mast with a reef knot.
- Pass the two halyards into the masthead hole and then through the fairlead of the figure-eight cleat. Don't forget the figure-of-eight knots at the ends.
- Fasten the sheets on the toggles of the booms. That's all. You are now ready to sail.

8-5. Both sails are furled onto the boom. The kayak is now ready to be paddled in a normal manner. (Photo courtesy Didier Plouhinec)

If There Is No Wind

Lower the sail and furl it on the boom. Using the sheet and a series of half-hitches, stow the sail and boom together. The boom is then passed under the chart elastics. A small elastic with a loop and ball-end stop works, too. With the sail thus stowed, you can paddle without any problem.

Side Wind or Strong Wind

You will use only one part of the sail.
- Unfurl the sail from the boom.
- Tighten the halyard to make a good backstay.
- Hoist the sail.
- Pull in the sheet slowly. The kayak will lean, so be ready to lean your body on the opposite side.
- Choose a side and extend your paddle as an outrigger (brace). If you are going downwind in a heavy swell, your partner will take the other side. If the wind is strong, your partner should brace on the same side.
- Always be ready to slacken the sheet and spill some wind.

8-6. In high wind conditions, one sail can be completely reefed onto the boom. (Photo courtesy Didier Plouhinec)

To Take a Reef

This is for high winds and only for a single sail. Remember that this is a kayak with a sail, not a real cutter! If you sail downwind and you want to reduce the sail, the angle between the mast and the boom will be closed and the boom will lift because your kayak has no boom vang. Reefing the sail is a solution only in strong side winds or when on a reach.

- Lower the sail and pull in the sheet.
- Undo the toggle from the clew.
- Fasten this toggle to the upper clew.
- Fold the lower panel of this sail and fasten the small toggle to the second reef point. See figure 8-6.
- Slacken the sheet and hoist the sail.
- Pull in the sheet again.

Downwind

Except in strong winds, sailing downwind is safe in a kayak. With the Aleut Sea II I have sailed up to 8 knots in a following sea. Because you cannot see anything, you must be in constant contact with your partner, who gives you the course to follow on your compass. A window in the sail might be a solution to this problem.

While the Aleut Sea II can sail unloaded, a fully loaded boat is safer for beginners.

Sailing into the Wind

With this rig the Aleut can sail 80 degrees to windward; good sailing boats, 30–35 degrees.

Kites

Ed Gillet, who started his ocean-going career as a sailor, converted a double kayak into a very passable ocean-going sailboat, by means of inflatable sponsons. To catch the wind, he attached a 15-square-foot parafoil kite to his bow. With this setup he made a successful crossing from Monterey, California, to Hawaii in 1987.

It takes practice and a certain amount of dexterity to launch and control a kite from a kayak, so you should experiment in safe conditions close to shore before heading for the open sea. Kites can be hand-held, but your kayak will be more manageable if you leave your hands free to steer or brace. For this reason, the kite's line should be allowed to slide along the deck, up toward the bow, either by a pulley system or by paying out a trip line. In this way your kayak will be pulled from the front.

It is important that the trip line be securely connected to the line that anchors the kite. It must be possible for you to pull the kite's line back within your reach and under your control. As a second line of defense keep a sharp knife secured to your life jacket, so you can cut the line if necessary. You can always retrieve your kite from the sea and live to fly it another day. Remember, a kite can only pull you downwind. If your giant parafoil cannot be disengaged, racing downwind at 8 to 10 knots toward weed-covered rocks could provide unique entertainment for the local beachcombers. On the other hand, an offshore wind could cause you or your next-of-kin great distress.

NAVIGATION

Navigation is a highly specialized subject, and the more ambitious your expedition kayaking, the more you should know. The following aspects are particularly useful to the kayaker.

Nautical charts are the basic tool for planning any kind of adventurous sea trip. They are the maps of the sea, and with only a little practice they will soon become a joy to look at and to use.

Scales

The relation between the distance on a chart and the distance over the surface of the earth is called the scale. The larger the scale of the chart, the smaller the area of the globe it will cover.

Chart scales can vary, but for coastal paddling a suitable scale would be between 1:50,000 and 1:150,000. If you fancy doing some harbor exploration, a scale of 1:10,000 would give you more local detail—the larger the scale on the chart, the more detail will be shown.

Normally charts are very accurate, but if you decide to explore some of the more remote areas of the world, you might find that the details given on the map bear little or no relationship to what is shown on the chart. Until I paddled along the Bering Sea coast of the Aleutian Islands, I thought that all nautical charts were scribed by the hand of God. It was only when I discovered that a river that was supposed to run into Blackstone Bay on Umnak Island did not exist that I realized that this was not the case.

A chart can be a little confusing at first glance because of all the tiny figures on the part of the chart that represents the sea. These are the depth soundings. On older charts the soundings are given in fathoms and feet (1 fathom equals 6 feet). Most charts today are metric, however, and print soundings in meters and decimeters (for example, 103 for 10.3 meters). All soundings on charts are taken from a point below which the tide is unlikely to fall, called the chart datum. This is the level of the lowest astronomical tide. On your chart you will find that dry land is shaded a buff color, but any area awash at high tide and dry at low tide is colored a nice seaweed green. These drying heights are also marked in meters and decimeters (underlined) and show the height above chart datum to which the area dries. It would be worth your while to obtain the booklet of chart symbols and abbreviations, sold where you purchase nautical charts.

Some information marked on the charts is of

direct interest to the ocean paddler. This includes any changes in depths, drying heights, and the quality of the sea bottom (possibly indicating a long walk in deep mud at low tide), tide races and overfalls, whirlpools, speed and direction of the tidal stream, types of shoreline, positions of buoys marking the navigation channels for large shipping, and conspicuous buildings and so on that can be used as transit markers.

To measure distance across the chart, use the scale at the side—one minute of latitude equals one sea mile. A long piece of fine, thin chain is good for laying on the chart to obtain distances because its flexibility will enable it to go in and out of small bays and around headlands. Use only a soft lead pencil so that any marks can be removed without spoiling the surface of the chart.

I find two set squares easier to use than a parallel rule. If you intend to use dividers, obtain a good pair with fine points—fingernail scratching on the edge of a torn-off cigarette packet is not really setting a good example in equipment preparedness.

Charts should be kept dry and in good condition. If you intend to carry yours on the foredeck directly in front of you, seal it inside a special transparent waterproof chart bag made for the purpose, or cut the chart into convenient-sized portions and cover each piece on both sides with a self-adhesive, transparent, waterproof covering.

If you intend to paddle in a wilderness area, I would recommend that you study the relevant topographical maps and include them in your equipment.

Bearings

On your chart you will see what is called a compass rose. The geographic or true north is parallel to the lines of longitude, which run from the top to the bottom of the chart. The compass you use on the deck of your kayak, however, will point to what is called magnetic north. The difference between this magnetic north and true north is known as the magnetic variation. This variation is not constant and it varies depending upon its position on the earth's surface or the passing of time. To discover the variation for the area in which you intend to paddle, you need only consult the appropriate chart. This variation will be printed on the compass roses that are placed strategically across the chart. You will see that it is expressed in degrees either east or west of the true north meridian. If you find that you have to convert a "true bearing" to a magnetic one or vice versa, follow these guidelines: magnetic to true—add the easterly variation; true to magnetic—subtract the easterly variation.

Remember that when you are heaping equipment upon your foredeck, your compass can be influenced by any close object that gives off a magnetic disturbance. Diving knives and transistor radios should therefore be kept away.

Tides

To the casual onlooker sitting on the beach, the water moved by the tide appears to travel only up and down the sand. Linked, however, with this rise and fall are the horizontal movements of the water. These are known as the tidal streams. Far out to sea these streams have little effect, but close inshore where most paddling takes place, their effect can be quite pronounced. By studying the tidal streams, however, and using them carefully, the ocean paddler can make these water movements do a good deal of the work for him. A tidal stream flowing parallel to a coastline can make a journey half as tiring. If the stream runs past a headland its speed will increase. It will slow down again as it runs along a bay. If the bay is well indented, be careful when you paddle close inshore lest you find yourself sweating against a back eddy that is running in the opposite direction along the shoreline. When paddling against the tide, these back eddies can prove very useful.

If, as you paddle along, you come across a place where a fast tidal stream crosses over an underwater shelf or ridge, you will see waves breaking steeply like those on a rapid river. This is called an overfall, and unless you are proficient at paddling in surf, this type of disturbance will prove very dangerous. If by some unfortunate mischance the wind happens to be blowing against the tide, you may find the conditions almost lethal.

The tidal streams that flow around some coastlines are complicated, but they flow in predictable patterns. Because these patterns are predictable, their direction and strength at different times can be published. Tide tables can be obtained from boat chandlers, and there are basically two sources where the speed of a tidal stream can be obtained: from a chart—small-feathered arrows show the flood stream and unfeathered arrows depict the ebb stream—and from a *Tidal Stream Atlas.*

The trouble with the information given in the *Tidal Stream Atlas* is that it gives only the speeds for areas several miles offshore. Charts, on the other hand, tend to show more localized tidal speeds, but a certain amount of experience is needed to work out exactly what will happen close inshore. There tidal movement is influenced by headlands, which will increase the speed somewhat, and the presence of islands, which tend to constrict the tidal flow and increase the speed even further.

Tidal predictions are not accurate because the times of high and low water can be influenced by such variables as barometric pressure, high winds, and (in an estuary) heavy rains and melting snows. Storm surges (caused by the passage of a sudden depression), such as those that occur in the southern North Sea, can oscillate the level of the sea. Coupled with gale-force winds and a tide that is abnormally high, storm surges can cause widespread flooding.

Tides (see fig. 9-1) are caused by the gravitational pull of the moon and, to a lesser extent, the sun. The moon and sun together exert their greatest pull when they are in conjunction (sun directly behind the moon—new moon), or in opposition (on opposite sides of the earth—full moon). The tidal range is greater at this period; and these are known as spring tides. When the moon and sun are at right angles to each other (in quadrature), there is a lesser influence and, consequently, a lesser tidal range, known as neap tides. Spring and neap tides occur every week alternately throughout the year.

On March 22 and September 22 or 23 annually, the sun crosses the equator, and its declination is zero. The spring tides occurring at this time are greater than normal, and you should take care if you intend to plan trips at this period, known as the "equinox" because day and night are equal.

Because tidal streams are faster flowing during spring tides, your passage will be easier and quicker with the tide or more difficult paddling against it. Any adverse conditions—for instance a wind blowing against the tide, or the stream rushing over shallows—will be worsened by spring tides.

On the open sea, a change in the direction of the tidal stream does not always coincide with the time of high water (HW) and low water (LW), and you may find the tide running in the flood direction perhaps as much as two hours after the ebb has started, or vice versa. The difference between HW and LW each day along the coast is six hours thirteen minutes. The time of HW is approximately fifty minutes later each day.

When the direction of the tidal stream changes, it is said to be "slack water," although this may not last for very long. The twelfths rule (see fig. 9-2) tells us that the level of water does not rise or fall at a constant rate throughout the six-hour period between LW and HW and between HW and LW. The greatest rate of rise or fall (and hence the

Charted height

Mean high-water springs

High tide

Present level

Height of high tide

Range of tide

Rise of tide

Low tide

Height of low tide

Drying height

Chart datum

Charted depth

Seabed

9-1. Tidal range

strongest tidal stream) occurs halfway through the tide in open water. In rivers and estuaries, the greatest rate occurs soon after the stream has commenced to run in the new direction.

Currents

There are also water movements within the sea, but their origins are thermal rather than lunar. Consequently their direction never changes. Currents have a much smaller influence on the sea paddler than do tidal streams.

Transits

The time-honored method of navigation by transits has two great advantages: It is simple and exact. For these reasons and because of the presence of objects, the system is of more practical use to the coastal paddler than any other. The principle is simply that of keeping two objects in line, one behind the other, and observing their movement in relation to each other. In figure 9-3 paddler A has the buoy in line with the lighthouse. Because the buoy and the lighthouse stay relatively in line with each other, he knows that he is drifting neither

Hour 1 ——————————— 1/12

Hour 2 ——————————— 2/12

Hour 3 ——————————— 3/12

Hour 4 ——————— 3/12

Hour 5 —— 2/12

Hour 6
└ 1/12

High water

Range
of
tide

Low water

Twelfths Rule
Hour 1 of rise or fall—1/12 of tidal range
Hour 2 of rise or fall—2/12 of tidal range
Hour 3 of rise or fall—3/12 of tidal range
Hour 4 of rise or fall—3/12 of tidal range
Hour 5 of rise or fall—2/12 of tidal range
Hour 6 of rise or fall—1/12 of tidal range

9-2. The twelfths rule helps the paddler understand the variation in the rate of rise and fall of tides.

one way nor the other. If, however, the objects appear to move apart from each other, he knows he is traveling or drifting in the direction that the marker farther away is opening up in relation to the nearer marker. Paddler B has observed that the lighthouse appears to have moved to the right in relation to the buoy; because of this he knows that he is drifting to the right.

It is particularly important to understand transits in order to determine whether you are making headway against an adverse wind or tide. The paddler in figure 9-4 has a hummock of grass lined up with hill A in the background. He is also using

a nearby hummock of grass lined up with hill B on the far headland. By watching these objects move in relation to one another, he can take heart that he is not standing still against the adverse conditions.

Any object can be used as a transit marker, and it is part of the art to change marks constantly as the need arises.

If you have to pinpoint your position over, say, a wreck or a reef, the intersection of straight lines drawn through two sets of transit markers will do the job exactly. As an ocean paddler, you should work at becoming transit-conscious as soon as

9-3. Transits help the paddler to determine whether he is making headway against winds or tides.

9-4. Any object can be used as a transit marker.

possible by relating the transit marks on your chart with the objects around you on the sea and on the land.

Buoyage

Anyone who paddles out onto estuaries or the open sea should become familiar with the various systems of buoyage that are designed to keep regular ocean traffic moving safely and smoothly in restricted waters. Buoyage can also help keep the seas free from upturned, empty kayaks. Knowledge of buoyage will help the ocean paddler locate his position accurately in bad conditions and will enable him to make decisions that take into account local shipping movements.

If you must enter busy shipping lanes, keep the intrusion to a minimum and cherish the thought that some ships take up to 10 miles to stop. Unless someone were looking over the side, he would not even know he hit you.

Ships turning around buoys at high speed will skid a considerable distance sideways. A wall of

steel and rivets approaching at, say, 6 to 10 knots can make even the bravest paddler feel uneasy. Make yourself familiar with the idiosyncrasies of local shipping movements so that you are not caught out.

Lateral Marks

In 1982 most of the maritime nations of the world signed an agreement sponsored by the International Association of Lighthouse Authorities with a view to standardizing aids to navigation. The United Kingdom and Europe subscribe to the Region A system (see fig. 9-5): port-hand day marks are red, starboard are green. All colors apply when approaching from seaward. (See the color code in fig. 9-5 inset.)

In 1983 the United States Coast Guard began modifications and, together with Canada, adopted the Region B system (see fig. 9-6). Port-hand day marks were changed from black to green—starboard-hand marks were already red—and white lights were no longer to be used on port or starboard navigation aids.

9-5. The International Association of Lighthouse Authorities maritime buoyage system for region A (the United Kingdom and Europe) shows cardinal and lateral marks.

Color code

Red	
Green	
Yellow	
Black	

DANGER FIRING RANGE

N

9-6. The International Association of Lighthouse Authorities maritime buoyage system for region B (the United States, Canada, and Japan) shows cardinal and lateral marks.

Color code

Red	
Green	
Yellow	
Black	

N

DANGER FIRING RANGE

Isolated Danger Marks

An isolated danger mark is a pillar or buoy over an isolated danger that has navigable water all around it. If an awareness of your position and of dangers is important during daylight hours, it is vital during the hours of darkness. Because of this, you should acquaint yourself with the most common light-flashing sequences and their chart abbreviations (fig. 9-7).

Isolated danger marks are coded as follows:

Topmark—Two black spheres, one above the other.

Color—Black with one or more broad horizontal bands.

Shape—Pillar or spar.

Light—White. Group flashing (two).

Safe Water Marks

Safe water marks indicate that there is navigable water all around the mark; these include center line marks and midchannel marks. Such a mark may also be used as an alternative to a cardinal or a lateral mark to indicate a landfall.

Special marks are yellow, but they are not normally of interest to the paddler unless used as a traffic separation mark where use of a conventional channel mark may cause confusion Sometimes a yellow buoy marks the seaward extremity of an army firing range.

Topmark (if any)—Single red sphere.

Color—Red and white vertical stripes.

▭	(F.) Fixed continuous light
▭◼▭◼▭◼▭	(Fl.) Flashing regular intervals
▭◼◼◼▭	(Gp. Fl.) Flashing in groups
◼◼◼◼◼◼◼◼◼◼◼	(V. Qk. Fl.) Very quick flash (100 or 120 per minute)
◼▭◼▭◼▭◼	(Qk. Fl.) Quick flash (50 or 60 per minute)
◼▭◼▭◼▭◼	(Occ.) Occulting light longer than dark
◼▭◼▭◼	(Gp. Occ.) Group occulting
◼▭◼▭◼	(Iso.) Isophase equal periods of light and dark

(Alt.) Alternating steady light, changing color
(Dir.) Directional light, a steady light
(Long fl.) Light not less than two-second durations

9-7. Common light-flashing sequences

Shape—Spherical, pillar with spherical topmark or spar.

Light (when fitted)—White, isophase, occulting or one long flash every ten seconds.

Channel Separation Marks

Channel separation marks are positioned where a channel divides. If the preferred channel is to port the description is as follows:

Topmark—Single green cone, pointed upwards.

Color—Green with a broad horizontal red band.

Shape (buoy)—Cone, pillar, or spar.

Light—Green. Composite group flashing (two plus one).

If the preferred channel is to starboard (System A) the description is as follows:

Topmark—Single red cylinder or can.

Color—Red with a broad horizontal green band.

Shape (buoy)—Cylindrical (can) pillar or spar.

Light—Color red. Composite group flashing (two plus one).

Cardinal Marks

Cardinal marks (see fig. 9-8) are laid to indicate that the deepest water is on the named side of the mark, or which is the safe side to pass danger; e.g., a north cardinal mark is passed to the north (i.e., you must leave the mark to the south of you). A kayaker may well do the opposite, and so avoid being in an area that larger vessels are navigating.

North cardinal mark:

Topmark—Two black cones, one above the other, points upward.

Color—Black above yellow.

Shape—Pillar or spar.

Light (when fitted)—White. Very quick flash or quick flash.

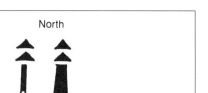

North

West

East

Area of interest

South

9-8. Cardinal marks.

East cardinal mark:

Topmark—Two black cones, one above the other, base-to-base.

Color—Black with a single broad horizontal yellow band.

Shape—Pillar or spar.

Light (when fitted)—White. Very quick flash (three) every five seconds or quick flash (three) every ten seconds.

South cardinal mark:

Topmark—Two black cones, one above the other, points downward.

Color—Yellow above black.

Shape—Pillar or spar.

Light (when fitted)—White. Very quick flash (six) plus long flash every ten seconds or quick flash (six) plus long flash every fifteen seconds.

West cardinal mark:

Topmark—Two black cones, one above the other, point to point.

Color—Yellow with a single broad horizontal black band.

Shape—Pillar or spar.

Light (when fitted)—White. Very quick flash (nine) every ten seconds or quick flash (nine) every fifteen seconds.

Coastal Problems

Reading Charts

With a little practice, a quick look at a chart should give you an overall picture of an area. Charts are designed for those who go to sea in much larger craft, and the ocean paddler must therefore cultivate an ability to read between the lines. Figure 9-9 shows what could be a typical and interesting piece of coastline for exploration.

An experienced kayaker looking at the chart on which figure 9-9 is based might make the following observations.

In a heavy swell, only the north end of the bay will give any hope of a trouble-free landing (fig. 9-9A). The approaches to the bay may be made more difficult by a race off the headland. If the bottom is shelving there will be an associated overfall. The small sheltered inlet on the south side of the island (fig. 9-9B) would make a good landing place, but if the island is a small one beware of the swell that sweeps around and causes rough water by colliding in the approaches to your landing place.

In an emergency only, the north end of the unprotected beach might be used by a proficient group (fig. 9-9C). The bay (fig. 9-9D) is dangerous—because of its size, the beach probably slopes steeply, causing dumping surf. In any sort of a swell, this bay could be used only in an extreme emergency and with great care. A harbor (fig. 9-9E) provides the classic protection for shipping, but very small craft should take time to study the approaches as best they can from the seaward. The north pier receives the main force of the

9-9. These are some typical coastal problems that the experienced paddler would foresee by studying a chart.

swell, which collides with the wall. The waves are then reflected directly back into the swells, which come up behind. The size of the swell will govern the size of dangerous clapotis (waves caused by the colliding walls of water). These areas are very hazardous, and you should steer well clear of them.

Take care as well when entering between piers (fig. 9-9F); there may be an extensive area of turbulent water known as the "bar" where the river

water meets the open sea (and probably a fast tidal stream). If you have taken time to plan your trip, you should enter the harbor on a flooding tide. If you have mistimed your entrance, however, you may have a battle against an ebb stream on your hands. When leaving the harbor, the south side of the pier would be best given a wide berth. Although not so violent as the direct clapotis, the angle of these reflected waves will cause the waves to peak up steeply and high, making your kayak pirouette on the crests, with perhaps most of your kayak hanging in fresh air—a good place to practice whitewater technique.

Fetch is the distance across open water over which the wind blows without hindrance (fig. 9-9G). The height of the waves caused by the wind is governed by the wind's speed and the fetch. If you are paddling a little way offshore, the fetch may be only a few hundred feet if the wind is coming from the direction of the shore, and even though it may be gale force the waves will be comparatively small. This is known as a weather shore. If the wind is blowing onto shore, this is known as a lee shore. The fetch could be many hundreds of miles, creating big surf and dangerous landing conditions.

The beach (fig. 9-9H) is an ideal landing place on a weather shore with a gently shelving beach and easy access inland.

In blustery weather all shoals and shallows (fig. 9-9I) must be viewed with caution. If the swells are large, shoals will be marked by breaking seas. Tidal streams also move faster over these shallow areas, and when these streams drain out between sandbanks they have a tendency to flow at right angles to the general direction you may have seen predicted in the *Tidal Stream Atlas*.

Take care when negotiating small isolated groups of rocks or pillars (fig. 9-9J) off exposed headlands, especially in heavy swells. They receive the full force of the tidal streams, which will increase in speed as the water flow is constricted. If the normal tidal streams are exceptionally fast, large and dangerous swirls and eddies can be caused after the stream has passed through.

Even when you have left the worst of the weather behind and think you are now paddling on sheltered waters, be especially careful at the base of mountains and high cliffs (fig. 9-9K). Localized gusts can hit downward with great violence, causing multiple capsizes among unsuspecting beginners.

Wind

Things are not always what they seem to be, and even the general direction of the wind can be deflected and contorted by the topography of the land. Nor should the general direction of the wind be confused with localized sea breezes, which will have far more effect on your paddling pleasure. The effect of these sea breezes is not usually felt more than 10 miles or so offshore. The cause is simple. The land is heated by the sun until its temperature is higher than that of the sea. The heated air over the land rises rapidly, causing the cool air over the sea to rush in and take its place (often with its accompanying fog).

These onshore breezes can be quite strong—a strong breeze on the Beaufort Wind Scale (fig. 9-10) has a mean wind speed of approximately 25 knots. Because many of these localized winds are predictable, the cautious paddler can time his trips accordingly by either utilizing the relative stillness of the mornings or evenings or by timing more long-distance expeditions on a seasonal basis and waiting for the spring or fall. In some areas, winter brings the most settled weather.

In contrast, katabatic winds blow offshore, and because of this they can be very dangerous to any small boat. These winds occur when cold air accumulates on snow-covered hills and mountains. The pressure builds up and any small change in atmospheric conditions releases this dammed up air, causing it to rush down the mountain slopes and out to sea. In the Aleutian Islands these winds are called williwaws, and it was these horrifying avalanches of cold air that caused a whole race of people to build their homes underground.

High coasts and cliff-lined shores bring their own problems, and what appear to be safe onshore winds can be deflected to blow parallel to the coast. You can also expect sudden wind shifts near islands and headlands.

Because wind is the ocean kayaker's greatest

enemy, a knowledge of the Beaufort Wind Scale is essential if any weather forecast you hear is to be interpreted correctly. This scale normally gives the Beaufort number, the speed range of the wind in knots, a description of the wind, the condition of the sea, and the probable height of the waves in meters. The wind direction indicates the compass quarter from which the wind is expected (e.g., a northerly wind blows from the north).

The Beaufort Wind Scale applies only to open water, and you may be paddling with a fetch of only 2 or 3 miles. (Fetch is the distance over which the wind blows unhindered.) The sea state in that case might be almost flat, even with a Force 8 gale. Therefore, to be of more use to the paddler, I have provided a table based on the formula for kinetic energy by which to make comparisons. You may be misguided into thinking that because you can cope with a Force 5 wind, you can also cope with a Force 6 wind—after all, it is only one unit up the Beaufort Wind Scale. The difference is considerable, however, and the pressure on the chest of the paddler if going into the wind is 220 units for Force 5 to 364 units during a Force 6. On

The Beaufort Wind Scale					
Beaufort Number	Speed (Knots)	General Description	Energy or Wind Pressure	Sea	Kayaker's Criterion
0		Calm.	0	Sea like mirror.	Suitable for initial training from "safe" beaches.
1	1–3	Light air.	4	Ripples appear.	
2	4–6	Light breeze.	18	Tiny waves. No breaking crests.	
3	7–10	Gentle breeze.	50	Small waves. Crests begin to form.	Life gets interesting for all. Good for practicing capsize drill. Getting tough for beginners.
4	11–16	Moderate breeze.	128	Medium waves building up. Some white horses.	About the limit for the proficiency test standard paddlers on journey.
5	17–21	Fresh breeze.	220	Decidedly lumpy sea. Many white horses.	Anybody over proficiency standard enjoys this. Usually creates very good surf.
6	22–27	Strong breeze.	364	Large waves everywhere. Continually white horses.	Short journeys by advanced kayakers all right, but you are reaching the border-line.
7	28–33	Near gale.	544	Sea piles up. Spindrift off tops of waves.	Surf tends to be big. Experts are beginning to swear.
8	34–40	Gale.	800	The difference from a landsman's view of these is difficult to say except that the sea looks lumpy, high breaking waves and spindrift following the wind path.	Surf gets to be very big, and you spend your time hanging on to your tent.
9	41–47	Strong gale.	1104		
10	48–55	Storm.	1512		Surf enormous, and you get blown away with your tent.
Formula for kinetic energy: $E = \frac{1}{2}MV^2$ when E = Energy, M = Mass, V = Velocity					

9-10. The Beaufort Wind Scale

my Beaufort Wind Scale, therefore, I have included a column for the energy or wind pressure that shows the energy ration of the wind or, more precisely, the pressure of the wind against the body of the paddler and kayak.

Fog

The most common type of fog is known as advection fog. It is caused by relatively warm air blowing over a cold sea, usually during the spring or summer months. Fogs such as this are often associated with cold currents like the Labrador and California currents. Unfortunately for the sea paddler, winds do not tend to decrease during these fogs, but in fact remain quite strong. Advection fog is different from radiation fog, which forms over land masses on cold windless nights and can extend 10 to 15 miles offshore. Radiation fog is usually dispersed by the heat of the morning sun.

It is important that you know the names of the different audible fog signals and be able to differentiate among them. It is not much good if you do not know whether the wailing you can hear through the fog is a typhon or a diaphone, especially if the chart tells you that the two signals are 10 miles apart!

When training advanced groups in fog, and the shore is invisible, have some well-qualified helpers with you. Every member of the group should carry a compass and a whistle or a hand-held fog horn. In case of emergency, each should have a compass bearing that will get him back to shore again. It is best if the leader carries a loud audible signal that his group can "home in" on.

Do not practice fog navigation in shipping channels. If you wish to keep shipping well clear of you and your group in an emergency, sound a "D" in Morse (i.e., one long blast followed by two short ones) and repeat this three times, then a two-minute pause and keep repeating. This signal will keep shipping clear of you if they are small enough to maneuver. But please note, it is not a distress signal.

Audible Fog Signals

Diaphone—(dia.) This is a powerful low pitch sound finishing with a deep grunt.

Siren—There are various types of sirens having different strengths and pitches.

Reed—This gives a feeble, rather high-pitched note.

Typhon—A strong medium-pitched note that sounds like a ship's fog signal.

Horn—Some wail, some give off sounds of different pitches combined together, others give a long steady tone while some seem to waver up and down. These sounds are very distinctive and once heard are easily remembered.

Whistle—(whis.) These are often worked by the swaying of the buoy. They can be shrill and clear, but if the swell is erratic the whistle will start and finish with a wheezing gasp.

Bells—Bells go ping, gongs go bong—some even go clonk—but you will be surprised just how far their sounds can carry.

The best way to learn about fog is to do a lot of exploring close to home.

Take time to familiarize yourself with your local sea area, especially in the area where most of your paddling takes place. There is no substitute for local knowledge. Get used to the sound, sight, and position of all the local buoys and especially the fog signals. Each of these signals usually has a sound or frequency different from nearby fog signals. One of the best illustrations of this is in the San Francisco Bay area. The bay is often shrouded in fog, and in the immediate vicinity of the Golden Gate Bridge there are about eight audible and assorted fog signals, which to the uninitiated ear can be very confusing.

Carry a compass and get used to the position of all local horns, whistles, sirens, and diaphones.

Carry some audible means of signaling your own position in case there is a danger of some less prudent water user colliding with your kayak. A whistle is adequate, but a fog horn is better. If all the members of a group have such signals, it becomes an easy matter to keep in contact with one another.

Cultivate a good sense of hearing. Take time to stop paddling and sit quietly and listen to the sounds, which are indications of land. Perhaps a dog is barking or there is the sound of surf rumbling upon rocks. From faraway comes the sound of distant traffic or nearby is the sound of the engines of a large vessel. Whatever the sounds, become aware of them and what they tell you about what is happening in your immediate vicinity. With practice the compass can be disregarded and fog navigation can become a matter of experience and instinct in local waters.

During times of poor visibility paddlers should maintain good group discipline and keep within communication distance of one another. Be careful especially close inshore on rocky coasts.

Global Positioning System (G.P.S.)

Obtaining a navigational "fix" has never been easy for the small boat skipper, and from a kayak it is almost impossible. There are a number of occasions when knowing your exact position might prove a blessing:

- On a lonely landfall when one needs to call for assistance.
- When out of sight of land either on a long open crossing or in prolonged bad visibility (i.e., you may wish to know if you are approaching a shipping lane).
- When passing through an unfamiliar, endless maze of small islands that all look the same and are adjacent to a very low and, therefore, invisible coastline.
- During long wilderness portages.

To solve all these problems, the space age has come to our help with a small, hand-held computer navigator known as a Global Positioning System (G.P.S.). Its operating principles are simple.

Orbiting the earth at a height of 22,500 miles are a number of evenly distributed, geosynchronous satellites. When you want to know where you are, you merely press a button. Your G.P.S. shoots a signal out into space, which is then bounced back simultaneously from three or more of these free-floating objects. The returned signal not only pinpoints your position but also calculates your ground speed and thus your estimated time of arrival at any given point.

The accuracy of this device is truly remarkable. The military version gives a position to an accuracy of within 4 feet. Because the G.P.S. is operated by the United States of Defense, however, the civilian version is subject to an accuracy deviation. It is therefore not accurate enough for an enemy to use it for missile guidance purposes, but it will still give you your position to within 20 feet. The sets are small enough to be held in the hand, and because they are waterproof they can be carried in a life-jacket pocket or even on the deck.

One final important message: For the G.P.S. system to be of any help to you on your travels, make sure that you *carry the appropriate chart!*

HAZARDOUS WILDLIFE

Many areas of the world have their own particular dangers. In this chapter I shall deal with only a small number in the hope they will inspire the would-be gypsy paddler into doing thorough research before departing for strange or inhospitable coastlines.

It will soon become apparent to you that there are any number of God's creatures just waiting to suck your blood, bite or sting you, and even eat you and your supplies. A number of examples come immediately to mind. Eskimo sled dogs have been known to eat camera cases with the film and leather boots and straps. Porcupines love salt and will devour any wooden paddles left lying about that are impregnated with it. Mice will eat their way through plastic bags to get at a food supply. While on the Aleutian Islands, we had either rats or squirrels (we never found out which) eat their way through a spray cover, then through a tent bag with a tent inside before helping themselves to our dehydrated food. The tent had to be repaired and the food reallocated—even small animals can create big problems.

Mosquitoes

If paddling takes you to the Arctic tundra, your life can be ruled by a tiny humming insect. The mos-

It will easily be understood that from his constrained position in the kaiak, which does not permit of much turning, the hunter cannot throw backwards or to the right. If, then, a wounded seal suddenly attacks him from these quarters, it requires both skill and presence of mind to elude it or to turn so quickly as to aim a fatal throw at it before it has time to do him damage. It is just as bad when he is attacked from below, or when the animal suddenly shoots up close at his side, for it is lightning-like in its movements and lacks neither courage nor strength. If it once gets up on the kaiak and capsizes it, there is little hope of rescue. It will often attack the hunter under water, or throw itself upon the bottom of the kaiak and tear holes in it. In such a predicament, it needs very unusual self-mastery to preserve the coolness necessary for recovering oneself upon even keel and renewing the fight with the furious adversary. And yet it sometimes happens that after being thus capsized the kaiak-man brings the seal home in triumph. (Nansen, Eskimo Life, *pp. 73–74.)*

mosquito is most active during the time you spend on land and not paddling—i.e., early morning and evening. These pests are at best unpleasant, but when they are present in large numbers they can be completely insufferable. Visibility is impaired by thick, impenetrable swarms. They can stampede a herd of caribou and drive people just about mad. Eating is a misery and, what is more, they can bite through quite thick clothing.

There are ways of keeping this menace at bay. If you know that mosquitoes are going to be a problem, make sure that your tent has netting at the vents as well as the door. If there is plenty of ventilation inside the tent, burn an antimosquito coil. The fumes from this are supposed to repel even the hardiest insect. You can, of course, smear your skin with any of the local special repellents, and there is even a tiny battery-operated device, which emits the high-pitched whistle of the male mosquito and is supposed to scare away the pregnant female—the one that does the biting. Every member of the group should have a head net. These are usually sold at stores and sports shops in mosquito areas. Thin cotton shirts are useless for protection. Treat mosquito bites by washing with cold, clear water and then bathing with calamine lotion.

Other Stinging Insects

It is hard to believe, but there are more deaths due to anaphylactic shock caused by insect stings than by scorpion or snake bites. People are usually aware that they are allergic to certain stings and bites, typically having had some bad experience in the past. If you believe you have such an allergy, you should take proper precautions and carry an Insect Sting Kit with you.

The Symptoms of Anaphylactic Shock

Within five to twenty minutes the patient will suffer breathing problems. A rash may occur. The nose and eyes may begin to run and soon the eyes will become swollen. The victim may feel sick and may vomit. The throat may swell and it will become impossible to breathe. This is a life-threatening situation, and *seconds* could mean the difference between life and death.

Treatment

The treatment of anaphylactic shock consists of hydrocortisone given intravenously in large doses together with epinephrine or a similar drug. If the distress in breathing is marked, it would be necessary for someone with sufficient training to cut into the trachea (windpipe) to make an artificial opening (tracheotomy).

Insect Sting Kits can be bought and should be carried as part of a comprehensive first-aid kit.

Anyone whose face starts to swell or who feels faint after an insect bite should seek the advice of a doctor immediately. Neither of these reactions, however, necessarily heralds anaphylactic shock.

Ticks

These are unpleasant little creatures that burrow into the flesh. Once dug in, only their rear ends stick out. There are a number of ways to withdraw these darlings. Use a suction cup (same as for a bee sting) or touch the tick with the hot end of a piece of wire or a blown-out match.

It is possible to remove ticks with long, fine-jawed tweezers, but take care not to leave the head behind, as the wound could become infected. If you can, first cover the tick with clear nail polish, which will suffocate it and make it easier to remove. Grasp the tick's head as close to the skin as possible and gently pull it straight out. Be careful not to squeeze the tick's body, as this may cause it to inject its fluid into you. Afterward, wash the bite area with antiseptic.

Someone once recommended touching a hot cigarette end to a tick, so I tried this on a harmless species that I had found busily burrowing into my stomach. It was not the best advice, because my skin started to sizzle before the hot end of the cigarette got anywhere near the back end of the tick.

Some North American ticks can be dangerous as well as unpleasant. The bite of a deer tick can inflict a bacterial infection known as Lyme disease. These little fellows are found in all types of vegetation and on animals, especially in the woods. Deer ticks are most active in the spring and autumn but are also present throughout the summer.

The disease has obvious symptoms. Within four to twenty days a ring-shaped rash may occur. The symptoms may also include fever, chills, headache, weakness and fatigue, and stiffness in the joints. In some cases there are no symptoms, while some common symptoms of Lyme disease may mimic those of arthritis. If you think that you have been bitten and have the symptoms, contact your doctor. If detected early, Lyme disease is usually treatable with antibiotics.

Recognize which tick is dangerous (fig. 10-1). You are looking for something tiny—about ¹⁄₁₆ inch wide—and orange-brown with a black spot near the head. The wood tick, which has white marks near its head, is about twice as big as a deer tick and is unlikely to give you Lyme disease.

Take precautions when camping in infested areas. Wear long sleeves and long pants tucked

10-1. Actual size of deer tick compared to 1 inch

into socks. Use an insect repellent and check your body constantly; get someone else to check your back. Brush off your clothing before going into your tent.

Scorpions

The first time I saw a scorpion, I was in Baja collecting stones to place around the valance of my tent. Scorpions, like snakes, love to crawl under things, so be warned. If you are in the desert and you need to move rocks or logs or you are collecting wood for a fire, use a stick as a probe first because you are probably disrupting a scorpion's home. If you know you are in scorpion country it will also pay to check your clothes and your boots before putting them on in the morning.

Of the three types of scorpions, only one is considered to be deadly. As a general rule, the smaller the scorpion the more dangerous the sting—and if it is also yellow in color you're probably in trouble. If you or one of your group is stung by one of the nondeadly varieties, the effect will be localized to the bite area. To determine whether what you're nursing is a deadly sting, tap the area lightly with your finger. If the victim feels

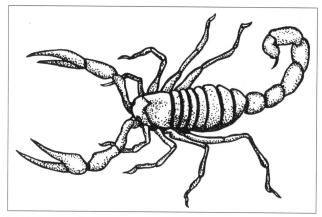

10-2. The scorpion

a tingly or prickly feeling traveling up the arm or leg toward the torso, then the sting is probably a bad one.

You must reassure the victim and *keep calm yourself.* The patient must *keep calm and stay still.* Do not let her walk about. If the sting is serious, the extremity of the limb will go numb. The patient may also complain of a restriction in the throat.

The patient needs a doctor. While you are waiting for help to arrive, apply a tourniquet to isolate the affected limb. Cold is the best treatment for a scorpion sting, so if you have any ice, a cold pack, or freon, apply it to the wound immediately. If you have no ice, any running cold water or a cold stream will have to do. This is a life-threatening situation and if I were unable to communicate with a doctor, I would not hesitate to pull the pin on my EPIRB (see p. 148).

Mice

Even the smallest of our little furry friends can make their presence felt in no uncertain way, as happened once to me on Vancouver Island. I had been paddling with a group in Johnson Strait,

enjoying views of killer whales. At the end of the day, we landed and made camp. To gain shelter from the light rain, I thought a cozy spot to pitch my tent might be a few yards in from the edge of the beach and in among the trees.

Before settling down for the night, I had decided to enjoy the luxury of a few squares of milk chocolate. I peeled off the wrapping paper, climbed into my warm sleeping bag, and then lay back and allowed two squares of the chocolate to dissolve slowly in my mouth. Unfortunately, those two squares sent me to sleep.

I awoke in the dark early hours of the morning, luckily having survived the obvious hazard of choking to death. I was still lying on my back, but I realized that what had woken me was a slight movement in the vicinity of the top of my head. The feeling was not unpleasant. It was as if an invisible hand were gently winding my hair around an invisible finger. My stupefied mind did not respond immediately to the gentle caress. Curiosity, however, soon got the better of me.

I slowly moved my hands round and into my hair. I felt a little lump wriggle between my fingers and discovered that something was busy making its nest in my hair. The lump then quickly disappeared out of my hand. In delayed shock, I sat upright as if I'd been shot and grabbed the light. As I shone it round, I was in time to see a tiny, comical-looking rodent with very large ears, leaving by a hole in my tent that had not been there before. A rustle on my other side enabled me to highlight and then identify my other visitor. It was yet another deer mouse and it exited through a hole of similar size on the opposite side of the tent. Of the four squares of chocolate that I had laid next to my bed the night before, a corner of each had been nibbled away.

As I lay back down to sleep in a tent that now appeared to have a musket-ball hole right through it, two thoughts drifted idly across my mind. Why, I wondered, couldn't those silly little mice have eaten just one whole square between them and left the other three squares intact for me?

The other thought made me feel uneasy. What would have happened, I wondered, if a *bear* had got a whiff of the chocolate? Any animal, large or small, will try to feed on your food droppings, so keep a food-free tent.

Porcupines

Porcupines like to eat wooden paddles that have been used in salt water.

Snakes

I shall not include what to do if you are being slowly swallowed by a boa constrictor; however, there are 30,000 deaths every year from snake bites, so I feel some information is worth including in this book. In the case of snake bites, the outlook is always good and most people recover completely except for cases in which the victim is bitten numerous times, has unusual sensitivity to snake poison, or is bitten near the heart; cases when there is undue delay or when no action is taken; and cases involving very old or very young people.

In Britain the snake problem hardly exists at all. The only poisonous snake that has its home in the British Isles is the adder, and you will see it only if your paddles take you to the more remote parts of Scotland or the Western Isles.

In North America there are a number of dangerous snakes you should be familiar with: coral snake, rattlesnake, cottonmouth (or water moccasin), and copperhead.

Prevention of snake bites is far better than cure, and there are some precautions that can be taken to minimize the risk of being bitten. Look where you are going when in snake country, and do not go prancing about in bare feet. Better still,

wear boots—the higher the better. Snow gaiters might be handy in this situation. When you are looking for wood, poke about with a long stick first and take care when you are lifting flat stones for the hearth or wandering through long grass. When paddling through swamps, look out for low branches and do not dabble your hands in the water while you are resting.

If you are bitten, remember the following:
- Do not panic—keep calm and do not run for help.
- Kill the snake by hitting it on the head with a rock, your heel, or a big stick, depending on its size, and keep it for identification. It may be needed afterward so that the right kind of serum can be administered.
- Apply a suction cup over the bite to draw out the poison. Fill a small glass bottle with hot water. Then empty out the water and place the neck of the bottle over the bite. As the bottle cools, the vacuum formed inside sucks the poison out of the bite.
- You need to know whether the snake is poisonous. Wash the blood away and check the wound carefully. Squeeze it to make the blood ooze out. If the blood shows from a number of small punctures arranged in a semicircle, then the bite probably is not poisonous. If, however, there are only two punctures, these are fang marks and more than likely the victim has been bitten by a venomous snake. But this is not a hard and fast rule—a weak bite from a nonpoisonous snake may leave only two puncture marks, and a hard bite from a poisonous one may leave several marks.
- You may have to apply a tourniquet, which should be loosened every twenty minutes for a one-minute interval. The patient should be observed closely, especially during this one-minute period.
- Keep the patient immobile and wash the wound with soap and water.

- Keep ice or cold water on the wound; this will reduce the speed at which the poison is absorbed into the bloodstream and also will reduce the pain.
- Treat the patient as for a fever. Keep the patient warm so that he perspires; this will get rid of body wastes and reduce the fever.
- If no medical help is immediately forthcoming, an adult should be given four tablets oral penicillin (if no allergy) plus four capsules 25 milligrams of Benadryl. Repeat two penicillin tablets every four hours.

How long it is before complications set in depends very much on how serious the bite is—how near to the heart, the age of the patient, and the amount of venom. With the bite from a pit viper, which includes the rattlesnake, cottonmouth, and copperhead, you have from half an hour to about four hours.

Bears

North America offers some wonderful coastline for ocean kayaking, and the coast of Alaska is the most beautiful I have ever seen. If, however, you choose to paddle along some of these coastal wildernesses, then very often you must be prepared to share this beauty with a very large animal. Its name is the brown bear, and although this great beast normally is quite happy eating berries, if it is surprised or provoked it will be equally happy to eat you.

Three types of bear inhabit North America: the comparatively small and quite numerous black bear, the polar bear, and the brown or grizzly bear. The grizzly lives well inland and is smaller than the coastal brown bear, which can grow to a staggering 1,200 pounds.

Brown bears, silvertips, or grizzlies—call them what you will—are really in a class by themselves.

They are the world's largest land carnivores and, furthermore, they can run at speeds of up to 30 miles per hour. But remember that bears are shy and would sooner avoid you if they are given the chance. They no more desire to bump into you than you desire to bump into them, but they do hate being surprised.

During the summer months, polar bears tend to move northward with the ice floes. Like the brown bear, these animals are highly dangerous killers and should be given a wide berth. Because polar bears exist where there are no trees to impede their line of sight, I would say that if you can see one with the naked eye and you are not paddling, then you are too close because they will also have you picked out.

Signs of Bear Activity

Bears have five toes with long claws on each foot (see fig. 10-3). They tread mainly on the front part of the forefoot so it is only on clear tracks in soft earth that you will see the complete sole. The size of the forefoot track depends on the age of the bear, but in a fully grown specimen it will be about 8 inches wide and approximately 11 inches long. The hind foot makes a print rather like that

Left forepaw   Left hind paw

10-3. Brown-bear tracks

of a barefoot man, except that on a bear the big toe is the shortest and smallest. The hind track of a fully grown brown bear is approximately 6 inches wide and 12 inches long. When a bear is walking normally, the hind foot is placed a good distance in front of the forefoot track.

Brown bear droppings are cylindrical in shape and about 6 inches thick. During the summer months they are found in large piles and consist of fur, bits of bone, and the remains of plants. When berry time comes around in the autumn, the feces are soft or liquid. When landing at dusk, it is a good thing to be able to identify bear droppings, especially fresh ones.

Precautions in Bear Country

Here are some ways to minimize a confrontation with a bear when you are forced to make camp in bear country:

- Do not pitch your tent too near a bear run. Look for long lines of footprints or flattened grass.
- Do not take shortcuts through alder bushes—bears love alder.
- Do not camp too near the mouths of salmon streams, especially if there are a lot of half-eaten salmon about. Look out for bear signs such as droppings or footprints.
- Never pass between a sow and her cub. If when you land you stumble upon a cuddly cub that looks all lonely and friendless, mummy will not be far away, so get back into your kayak and leave—in a hurry!
- Do not take strolls during the hours of darkness.
- Bears associate humans with food. Do not attract them by keeping a dirty and sloppy campsite.
- Do not leave foodstuffs around the campsite and do any cooking well away from the tents.
- Do not eat or store any food in your tent (including gum or chocolate).

10-4. Alistair Wilson and I compare the size of bear footprints while the sound of their growls can be heard from nearby alder bushes. I am carrying a Remington shotgun, for protection only. The weapon had a folding stock that made it easy to carry inside the kayak. For a month, I kept the gun cleaned and well oiled. It never occurred to me to do the same for the ammunition. During the last days of the trip, we finally got around to trying the gun on some small pieces of floating ice, and we discovered that some slight corrosion around the brass base of the cartridge cases prevented them from being ejected. (Photo courtesy Tom Caskey)

- Store any foodstuffs out of reach. Substances that have a fairly neutral smell, such as freezedried and dehydrated foods that are packed in plastic, can be kept in the sealed watertight compartments of kayaks. Any other

10-5. In bear country, sling your edibles well out of reach. A minimum safe distance would be to choose two trees approximately 3 paddle lengths apart. Sling your bags at least 1½ paddle lengths from the ground. These precautions, however, will present no problem for a squirrel.

10-6. If you have only one tree from which to hang your food bag, make sure it swings 1½ paddle lengths from the trunk, 1½ paddle lengths from the ground, and, if possible, the same distance down from the branch.

food should be bagged and hung high in the air on a line slung between two trees. (I have known a bear to tear off a spray cover to get a chocolate that was left in the cockpit while totally ignoring food stored elsewhere in the kayak.)

- Make plenty of noise when you land—talk loudly, whistle, sing, or bang the deck of your kayak. If you must wander about in bear country, try to let the animals know you are coming. Some people suggest bells fastened to clothing, others advocate rattling small stones inside tins.
- At night, keep a flare inside your tent; this might help scare away any bear who becomes too inquisitive.
- Mark the boundaries of your territory, even if it is only a one-night stop. Most animals do this, and the method is simple. Just urinate where any tracks lead to your campsite or at any gaps in the foliage where you think an animal might wander in. If signs of bear abound, as an added precaution you could urinate around your tent.

If the worst happens—and it might—there are no signs that indicate if a bear is about to charge. In the case of a close encounter, quietly talking while slowly backing away has been known to work. As you move, try to get out of the bear's line of sight behind a tree or boulder. If you are trying to escape a brown bear and there is a tree nearby that can be climbed, climb it quickly because the bear will not be able to follow you. The smaller black bear, however, can climb trees and will follow you up. If the bear charges and you have no way of defending yourself (and you certainly will not outrun a bear), I am told the best way to escape death or a bad mauling is to feign death. Lie on the ground and curl up into a ball with knees up and hands clasped behind your neck. Bears kill by biting the back of the neck or the throat, or by disemboweling; however I am told that if you can lie still and suffer the first few blows and bites without screaming out, the bear may consider you no longer a threat and leave you alone.

An old trapper once said to me, "The guy who goes out into the bush without the means of getting his dinner or defending himself is nuts!" Considering this, it would be prudent to carry a suitable firearm when in bear country. Not everyone thinks this way, and I remember being quite disturbed by the opinions of some of my paddling companions one evening as we sat talking around the dying embers of a campfire. To my dismay, I discovered that there are a large number of people who would not kill a bear even if this were necessary to save their own life, or the life of someone else in the group. For those who support this view, there is a less violent and certainly less permanent option.

In response to the increase in violent street assaults, pressurized containers of capsicum peppers can now be purchased in the United States. Sprayed in the face of a mugger, or in this case a bear, this substance causes blindness and severe pain. It has the same effect as that of having hot fat thrown in the face. These painful and blinding effects last for about twenty minutes, after which time the eyes and skin are supposed to revert back to normal. Those who have experimented on charging bears (how *do* people get these jobs!) assure us that it has the same effect on animals and even the most belligerent bear will turn around and make off in a hurry.

I must confess to the reader that I have not yet tried this for myself. I can see it would take considerable courage to wait until a charging grizzly bear has approached near enough for the spray to have its maximum effect. Those with weak nerves and an itchy trigger finger could well find themselves discharging their canister before the advancing mountain of fur is even within range. I can also envision problems in strong winds, especially if a bear is romping toward you with the wind at its back. It would seem that with regard to bears, prevention is definitely fraught with less risk than the "cure."

Alligators

A story that appeared in *Canoeing* magazine tells of how, on one December day, about 7 miles north of Florida's Silver Springs boat ramps, a competitive paddler named Dave Phillips found to his delight that he was leading the Oklawaha River Kayak Race. At a point where the river is about 60 feet wide, he saw an alligator on the surface right in the center of the river. The alligator, which appeared to be 8 to 10 feet long, turned and began to swim toward him. About 20 feet from the paddler, hissing and grunting, the gator opened its jaws wide. Phillips, who was still approaching at about 7 mph, shouted at the beast in an attempt to scare it off.

He then tried to turn the kayak away by twisting his body so that the hull would be presented to the gator, which by this time was attempting to snap at him in the cockpit. As it did so, he capsized and came out on the side away from the gator's jaws, which were sliding along the fiberglass hull. Phillips's 30-foot swim to shore was accomplished in record time. By now the gator had released the kayak and was floating alongside it. As the next competitors approached, the gator submerged.

The incident ended without bloodshed on either side. Phillips, much shaken, retrieved his boat, patched it up with duct tape, and paddled on to finish second. The gator had left its mark, however; its jaws had crushed a part of the top deck and put a number of tooth holes in the hull.

As no one was hurt, this incident was not considered an attack. A Fish and Game officer later apologized for the alligator, saying that it probably mistook Phillips for a 17-foot-long, yellow-and-white swimming deer!

The best way to explore the waterways of Florida is undoubtedly by sea kayak. There are, however, a million alligators in the state. They are protected by law, and their numbers are increasing. Since alligators *do* eat people, it is important to observe a few simple precautions in areas where alligators are known to live.

- Exercise extreme caution when landing. Alligators blend into the background so as to be almost imperceptible.
- Camp only on the raised platforms provided by the park service; otherwise, sleep in a tree! Bear in mind that alligators feed at dusk and at night.
- Do not tease them or throw food to them.
- Beware of the seemingly harmless small baby alligators. They have a nasty bite, and mother is probably nearby looking for the next meal.
- Do not imitate the alligator's *ugh, ugh, ugh* sound when in one's presence. This is the sound made by an alligator in distress, and it encourages all other adult alligators to come to its assistance.

Jellyfish

As a general rule most of the large, colorful jellyfish will give you a sting, and so will some of the smaller ones. Jellyfish have a histamine sting that causes irritation and burning at the point of contact. You will feel as if your skin has been beaten with stinging nettles.

Some people are allergic to histamine stings, and if this is the case, there may be a tightness in the victim's chest during the few hours after contact. The victim may have difficulty breathing and may even faint and collapse. If this happens, you need a doctor as soon as possible.

Prevention is better than cure, of course, and you should give all colorful jellyfish a wide berth whether they are floating or stranded on the beach, whole or in bits.

If the worst has happened, wipe away any part of the jellyfish still clinging to the skin, but *not with your hands*. Use a cloth or sand or salt water. Apply an antihistamine hydrocortisone cream or lotion. If you are on a surfing beach, a bystander or one of your companions may have some antihistamine tablets for hay fever for use if the patient's respiration becomes difficult.

Portuguese Man-of-War

The Portuguese man-of-war (also known as the Blue Bottle) is dealt with separately because it is certainly in a class of its own (fig. 10-7). Unlike most jellyfish, it is not just unpleasant, it is a killer. Because of this it is well that you know something about it and are able to recognize it on sight.

It moves across the surface of the sea by means of a gas-filled bladder, which is blown by the wind, and it looks like a sail, protruding above the water. The bladder is not large (it is about 6 inches long) and is pale blue in color with a touch of pink. From this float a complicated system of tentacles hang down to a length of more than 45 feet, and each of these tentacles is equipped along the whole of its length with row upon row of minute, barbed, flexible hypodermic syringes. Each one of these can inject a highly toxic poison. As these long fronds hang limply down in the water, all the tiny barbs are coiled up ready and waiting for the unsuspecting touch of a victim. The moment these tentacles are brushed against, the harpoons shoot out and cling with horrifying results.

To get some idea of the Portuguese man-of-war's power, I spoke to a young man whose legs had become entangled in the tentacles while swimming. He described the agonizing pain he suffered as like having red-hot wires wrapped around his legs. He spent nearly six months in a hospital, and at one time it was thought that his legs might have to be amputated. Years after, the evidence is there for all to see in the form of scar

10-7. The Portuguese man-of-war

10-8. The sea wasp

tissue that spirals around his legs from his ankles to the top of his thighs.

To treat Portuguese man-of-war stings, first rinse the affected area with methylated spirits or medicinal alcohol. Then with great care remove any stinging tentacles that may still be adhering to the skin. Do not touch them with your bare hands. After you have done this, rinse the area again with methylated spirits or alcohol.

If the sting area is extensive, you will need to obtain medical help as quickly as possible. Meanwhile, treat the victim for shock. There may be respiratory difficulties or failure followed by cardiac arrest, in which case administer mouth-to-mouth resuscitation and massage the heart. The patient will also need painkilling tablets.

Sea Wasp

The sea wasp is a truly deadly inhabitant of the sea, and because of its translucence it is difficult to see (fig. 10-8). Normally the bell of this jellyfish is not large, only about 8 inches high. The four clumps of tentacles that hang down, however, can be several yards long. Some specimens are known to have grown much larger.

The sting from this creature is extremely venomous, and if you are severely stung your life expectancy could be measured in minutes rather than years. Even a sting covering a very small area is excruciatingly painful, and the effects can last for ten hours or more.

The severity of the sting is in direct proportion to the size of the animal, and swimmers have been known to swallow tiny sea wasps accidentally without any lasting harmful effects. Luckily for most of us, this horror only affects those who kayak in certain parts of the Pacific Ocean and the northeast coast of Australia. It has been discovered that ladies' pantyhose provide very good protection, and I am told that quite a number of Australian lifeguards protect their legs in this way.

If you or someone else is stung, get medical assistance immediately. It has been found that applying vinegar gives relief from the pain. Give pain-killing tablets and treat for shock. If no vinegar is available, wash the affected parts with cold, clean water.

Sharks

All predators need to protect themselves from any damage that would disable them or limit their efficiency. It is for this reason that sharks close their eyes as they open their mouths to bite. It may also explain why, over the years, divers have found that a sharp blow inflicted anywhere on a shark's body, but especially on its snout, is enough to make it think twice about making an attack. If a kayak paddler is to benefit from this knowledge, he needs some implement that can deliver an immediate blow to an inquisitive shark, but that is also portable and can be wielded safely from the cockpit of his kayak.

A bang stick (fig. 2-12, p. 29) has the disadvantage of being highly specialized. It is not easy to inflict a positive hit with the first attempt. A glancing blow, which is no deterrent, is more likely, and the kayaker can then find himself in a more dangerous position. Because the bang stick is itself a potentially dangerous piece of equipment, it will need to be put on and taken off the deck before and after every trip. When the big moment arrives, the bang stick may well prove to be a rusty relic or even to have been forgotten altogether.

What is needed is an implement that can be carried as part of the kayak's permanent equipment and that preferably could lie alongside the spare paddle. After consulting with sport fishermen and others who have come into unwelcome contact with sharks, I offer the following suggestion, which I have called the panic prod.

In its simplest form, it consists of a piece of hardwood, round in section, about 1½ to 2 inches in diameter, and about 3 feet long. It has a loose shock-cord wrist loop at one end and a 3-inch spike at the other. The spike is a simple non-barbed type to allow the fish to pull free from the prod as it swims past. The paddler is therefore at considerably less risk of unwillingly accompanying the shark. Although not the perfect answer to a frightening problem, the panic prod is based on the well-known principal of "any port in a storm," and I feel sure it might well give paddlers a means of escape from all but the most determined of shark attacks.

Killer Whales

Although orca is no longer considered a threat to human beings, I feel I should include the killer whale on my list of dangerous wildlife—just in case someone new to the sport is frightened out of his wits the first time one pops up near his kayak. My own first experience paddling with killer whales goes back to the time when no one was quite sure what would happen if you came across one while paddling. This, of course, was before we locked these poor creatures up in soundroof, water-filled cages and condemned them to a lifetime of sensory deprivation, merely so that we could pay to watch them perform.

When you encounter an orca on the open sea for the first time, your reaction will probably be one of fear. I know the first time I was confronted by one of these then-unknown creatures, and at close quarters, I certainly felt a twinge of fear, especially when it moved in close and began to examine *me*. But after a few minutes, a kind of heart-pounding humility took over. This was an experience I shall never forget. Who knows, per-

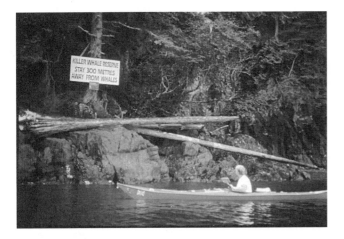

10-9. In order to prevent humans from "harrassing" the aqautic wildlife, this notice stands as a warning at the entrance of Robson Bight off Canada's west coast. (Photo courtesy Will Norby)

haps as it did me, the awe and beauty of it all will bring tears to your eyes.

Depending upon where you are, you may find that killer whales bring quite unexpected and sometimes unpleasant problems in their wake, though not of their own making. I experienced an encounter of this kind some years ago in Robson Bight, off Vancouver Island.

I was with a group from the Washington Kayak Club camping on the island. Robson Bight is well known for the large numbers of whales that frequent the area, and we were there to paddle with them as much as we could. The day in question was dull and windless. We had hired some hydrophones so that we could hear the whales as well as see them. Every now and again we would have to paddle in order to change position and keep up with our pod of about ten whales as they moved slowly south.

Our unwelcome visitor, when he arrived, was driving an aluminum whaler propelled by a very loud and smoky outboard motor that would have driven a boat three times as big. To a killer whale, who sees by sonar and whose delicate and sensi-

tive audio system can pick up messages from friends hundreds of miles away, the loud rasping roar of that engine must have been ear-shattering.

The man roared past our whales, then steered around sharply and churned in among the kayaks. It passed through my mind that perhaps he hoped he might capsize somebody. He shouted at no one in particular but he looked very angry. He gestured with his free hand toward the horizon. "Get away . . . clear off, you're harassing the whales!"

His boat never seemed to stay still. Over the noise, I tried to explain what we were doing and that we were being very quiet and circumspect in relation to the wildlife. While I was talking, he swirled and roared round and in and out between us. I also pointed out that I felt he was a greater harassment to the whales than we would ever be. I drew his attention to the fact that the local fishermen had a complete disregard for the welfare of the whales and appeared to be riding right over the feeding animals. I pointed out to him that they were actually running the animals down, in order to fill their nets with the very meal that the whales were enjoying.

This obvious truth seemed to infuriate him even more, and he snarled out that the whales were used to the fishermen and that *we* were the ones who were causing the trouble. In order to carry on with our conversation, the man had to bring the boat to a standstill. He still, however, punctuated every three words or so with noisy twists of the throttle. The now-established hostile tone of the conversation continued with his suggestion that we, as "foreigners," should all "clear off" back to our own countries. This remark brought a smile to a few tense faces. Sadly, the overall tone of my conversation with the supposed guardian of the whales did not improve, and he eventually sped noisily off, shouting inaudible parting shots over his shoulder.

I am still of the opinion that kayakers do no harm to the whales. Looking back on my own frequent close encounters with killer whales and remembering the times that the top of the fin has been *above my head*, I do not honestly feel that *I* have ever had *them* worried in any way. We probably give them something to talk about. Anyone attempting to "harass" a killer whale from the cockpit of his kayak is something I find difficult to imagine. Of course, if you wish to hear the whales laugh into the hydrophone, you could always try swearing at them and splashing with your hand.

It has been suggested that killer whales might feel crowded by kayaks. But consider the volume and speed of the kayak, which moves on a flat plain, and compare it to that of the whale, which, like an albatross, inhabits *vertical* space. I am sure you will agree that it is most unlikely that any orca that finds itself near a group of kayakers is going to suffer from an attack of claustrophobia. In my view, a killer whale is concerned as much by the presence of kayakers as a sparrow would be when a hang glider passes high overhead.

Don't Play the Fool with Wildlife

This heading sounds so obvious that the advice is almost on a par with "don't eat the daisies," but don't be smug. Of course all of us brave and sensible outdoors people know that it is neither adultlike or safe to poke the scorpions, tease the snakes, or smear honey on a child's face in order to get a good photograph of a bear licking it off— yes, that actually happened in Yellowstone National Park.

The trouble is, your kayak is going to take you away from your normal rational surroundings and into some strange and wondrous places. In these circumstances rationality can so easily go out of the window, and it is quite easy for you to be overcome by that peculiar local magic that can transform the most cautious paddler into a complete idiot. We can all fall into the trap. I remember running down to the water's edge on a small bay in Alaska, drawn by the sight of some killer whales that were swimming offshore. The sun was setting and I was dressed ready for bed in thin fiberpile long johns. The kayaks lay on the beach with their hatch covers removed. In spite of this and overcome with excitement, four of us jumped quickly into the boats and paddled out without life jackets or spray skirts, in order to chase after the whales. And this was in the days when we all thought orcas ate people! What the press would have done with any subsequent accident does not bear thinking about.

The following little story illustrates the problems that can arise when fooling about with even the mildest of wild animals.

My companions and I were paddling in southern Florida. Larry, our guide, was brought up in the area and is a well-known kayaker. He is a sensible, no-nonsense type of person and it was he who led us up the Loxahatchie River. As we nosed our way across the still water and alongside banks tangled with mangroves, Larry enlivened our trip with a running commentary on the local fauna. At lunchtime we pulled our kayaks up through a gap in the mangroves and sat down to eat our goodies.

I commented that spaced liberally around the site were lots of oval-shaped holes that looked as if they'd been dug by rather wide, flat rabbits. It might be more accurate to say the shape of the openings resembled the cross-section of an inverted soup plate. The mystery was soon solved when one of the inhabitants decided to show itself. A bored looking tortoise about 9 inches high and about a foot wide appeared at the entrance to one of these subterranean homes. His front door was at the base of an earth cliff about 18 inches high. On top of this small mound was a thorn bush. Although the tortoise had little space around its shell near the entrance, I noticed the hole seemed to fit its shape exactly farther down inside. The rim of the inverted soup plate was where its flipper-like legs stuck out at the side. The creature didn't leave the protection of its home completely but stood at its front door in order to observe the newcomers.

Noting my curiosity, Larry turned to me and lapsed into guide mode. "It's a gopher tortoise. Have you ever seen one?" I admitted as far as I was concerned the creature was a complete novelty. Larry moved toward the hole. "Here, I'll let you get a closer look!" He bent down and squeezed both hands tightly into the hole on both sides of the tortoise and grasped the shell. His idea was to lift the sleepy looking fellow out into the light and give us all a closer look. This is where things started to go wrong.

The tortoise decided it wanted no part of this and began to retreat backwards down its hole, ably assisted by four very powerful short legs.

Larry's hands were jammed tightly between the edge of the shell and the side of the custom-made hole. A hush fell on our little group as we realized that we were being entertained by something quite unusual. Larry's face started to go red as he pulled against the backward movement of the tortoise and slowly and surely we realized that he was being drawn down the hole by the tortoise. All this time, Larry courageously continued his informative chat. "These creatures build their homes in bank sides," he gasped. He was sweating profusely now and his face was even redder. Larry is a powerful man, but at this stage it was odds on for the tortoise. His forearms vanished first, then ever so slowly his elbows were lost from view. No longer crouching now, he had been obliged to topple forward onto his knees.

We all wondered what would happen. One thing we did know—the tortoise wouldn't be able to pull Larry *all* the way down the hole. Things were now at an impasse. Larry's arms were as far down as they would go and his face was pressed firmly against the thorn bush. He had stopped talking. By this time, he obviously needed all his breath for the battle with the tortoise. We watched in awed silence. He had blood on his face now, and he didn't have much choice but to keep on pulling. I wondered what the headlines would read. "Local man dragged to death by tortoise . . . earth moving equipment used to locate body!"

Whether the tortoise took pity on Larry or whether it had just about had all the fun it could take for one day, we will never know. Larry's bloody face slowly cleared the thorn bush and equally slowly, his clay-caked arms, still clutching the tortoise, slowly emerged from the hole.

Larry released the tortoise and wiped away the blood, and our ponderous and perplexed friend slowly returned to its home. Did I see it shaking its head? It was probably wondering why such a very large human creature tried so hard to enter its tiny living room.

I have now entered the gopher tortoise on my list of animals that can endanger life.

The moral: *Leave the wildlife to its wild life.*

EMERGENCY AID

Cramp

Cramp is a very painful condition caused by the sudden and agonizing contraction of a muscle or group of muscles. It can stop you walking, paddling, swimming, or even breathing, depending on which muscles are affected. If you are in the wrong place when you get an attack of cramp, you could even finish up dead.

This sudden muscle contraction can be brought about in a number of ways:

- By exertion and chilling from wind and water.
- By keeping a limb immobile in an unnatural or unusual position.
- By a poor sitting or footrest position. With novices, cramp is often caused by undue anxiety and tension (group leaders take note).
- By a salt deficiency in the bloodstream.

Relief from cramp can be obtained only by straightening and exercising the affected limbs. If the cramp affects the lower part of a paddler's body or legs, the patient must raft up between two others and then either stand up, supported by them, or lie along her own reardeck with her feet out of the cockpit. In this way, limbs can be easily flexed and good circulation restored. Whether the victim stands up or lies down depends on how rough the sea is.

If the cramp is persistent, the sufferer should be taken to shore or a capsize may occur—especially if the condition is due to tension.

Tenosynovitis

This is the kayaker's horror, and when it hits there is certainly no mistaking it. There will be a swelling of the forearm, and if you open and close the fingers you will hear a horrifying grating sound, like the creaking of new leather. It also hurts. Place your fingers on the offending spot; it is easy to feel the roughness of the moving tendon.

What has happened is very simple: The overactivity of the flexor tendons at the wrist have caused a swelling inside the tendon sheath. Hence the feeling that the tendon is being gripped by lumpy sandpaper as it moves inside the arm.

This painful condition is caused by unaccustomed activity or prolonged strain, and even experienced kayakers can fall victim to tenosynovitis after a long and grueling paddle, especially if conditions have been unexpectedly severe. Towing someone over a long distance can also cause this, so group leaders should make sure that any towing problem is shared by a number of people, no matter how strong and heroic the volunteers say they are.

The initial treatment for tenosynovitis is simple but drastic for the kayaker. The arm needs rest, so paddling must stop and the arm should be strapped up for one to three weeks. Do not be tempted to paddle in spite of the pain, as this could be dangerous. If the condition is ignored for even a short while, it could take up to three months to cure as well as an operation to free a tendon that may have adhered to its sheath.

If this happens on an expedition, the patient can do no more paddling and will have to be towed back to civilization. If the wrist and forearm are put in a splint, however, it may be possible for the patient to assist the person towing by steering and perhaps paddling a little from time to time.

Fishhooks

Fishhooks can be very nasty, but it might not even be one of your own hooks that does the damage. I have seen a paddler caught on the forehead by a hook that was left hanging from the branch of a tree by some careless angler. The hook cannot be extracted the way it went in, so push it forward until the barb breaks back out through the skin (fig. 11-1A). Cut the hook with pliers or wire cutters either where the hook entered or where it comes out (fig. 11-1B).

For those of us who leave our pliers next to the bicycle, there is a way of removing the hook without tools. All you need is a piece of string (fig. 11-2). In the absence of string you might have to revert to some of your fishing line.

Make a 12-inch loop out of a piece of string or cord. Loop this round the curve of the hook. Hook your index finger through the other end of the loop. Push down on the shaft of the hook. This

11-1. Removing a fishhook

11-2. The string method

will disengage the barb. Keep the string in line with the hook's long leg, then pull on the string until the hook emerges from its entrance hole.

Mouth-to-Mouth Resuscitation

Anyone who needs mouth-to-mouth resuscitation will not look pleasant as he lies upon the sand. The color of the face will be gray or white. The lips and ears will be dark purple, and a yellow froth may be coming from the mouth, together with bits and pieces of the patient's last meal. There are very good reasons, however, why you should fight back nausea and use mouth-to-mouth resuscitation.

The advantages of this method of artificial respiration are as follows:

11-3. Mouth-to-mouth resuscitation

- It can be started sooner than any other method—for instance in the water or across the deck of a kayak.
- Oxygen gets into the victim's lungs quicker than with any of the manual methods.
- The carbon monoxide contained in the rescuer's expired air can trigger the patient's own natural breathing.
- The patient is in the correct position should the rescuer need to administer cardiac massage.
- The rescuer can watch to see if the victim's face changes color and can watch the rise and fall of the chest.
- The rescuer has both hands free and can insure that the victim's airway is clear.
- No special equipment is needed.

To apply mouth-to-mouth resuscitation, first lay the patient flat. If there is time, position his head higher than his stomach. This should keep the fluids in the stomach. If the victim vomits, twist him over onto his side at once; otherwise he will inhale the vomit and choke.

Next, clear the mouth. Put your fingers in and check for dentures, bits of seaweed, or other obstructing material.

Then tilt the patient's head back. This should be twisted back as far as it will go, so that the chin sticks out (fig. 11-3A).

Make an airtight seal. This is done by opening your mouth wide enough to make a seal over the victim's nose and then blowing (fig. 11-3B). Use the hand that is supporting the chin to keep the victim's lips together.

If the nose is blocked, use the hand that is supporting the chin to open the victim's mouth. Open your mouth wide and make a seal over his mouth, then blow. If some air escapes from the victim's nose, either pinch his nostrils together or press your cheek against his nose. As you blow, watch out of the corner of your eye to see if his chest rises.

After you have blown into the patient's mouth, turn your head away and allow the air inside his lungs to escape. At the same time you can observe his chest go down. Start resuscitation with four to five quick inflations, then blow in time with your own breathing (twelve to fifteen times a minute).

All being well, the patient's color should soon look more healthy—he should have red lips and pink cheeks. You must continue with mouth-to-mouth resuscitation until he is breathing on his own again—no matter how long this takes—or until a doctor tells you to stop. When the patient recovers, treat for shock.

There are several reasons for using mouth-to-nose instead of mouth-to-mouth resuscitation. It reduces the risk of air entering the stomach because the nose reduces and directs the air that otherwise would be forced into the stomach. This means there is less possibility of vomiting, so it is ideal for drowning cases. It is easier to make an airtight seal over the nose with the mouth. There might, however, be problems if the victim has a history of sinus trouble or has a cold.

If by some mischance the patient's chest does not rise when his head is bent right back and his mouth is clear, you have a stoppage. Very quickly, turn the patient over onto his face with his arms above his head. Place your feet astride his waist and lift him, then move your feet together so that he is trapped between your knees. Pull his head back, by the hair if necessary. This will give you a straight airway. Give him a hard pushing blow two or three times between the shoulder blades. This should dislodge any obstruction and enable you to continue with mouth-to-mouth resuscitation.

If the victim's stomach rises up while you are administering mouth-to-mouth resuscitation, this is a sign that air has found its way inside. You must press on the air bulge gently but firmly so the wind comes out. This will probably cause the patient to vomit, in which case turn him over so that his head is on one side.

Dangers of Fresh Water

With mouth-to-mouth resuscitation every second is vital. The urgency is greater, however, when fresh water is involved. Any fresh water that gets into the lungs is absorbed into the bloodstream very quickly. This will dilute the blood and affect the heart rapidly. Salt water, on the other hand, is not absorbed into the blood at all, which means that the heart is not affected so quickly.

As a general rule, in fresh water a victim is thought to be beyond help after being immersed for three minutes, whereas with salt water there is hope of resuscitation even after the victim has been submerged for as long as five minutes.

Raft-Assisted Resuscitation

Using kayaks rafted together, mouth-to-mouth resuscitation can be carried out as easily on water as on land (fig. 11-4). Probably the best way to go about this is for the rescuer in the boat nearest the victim to turn around so that he is turning in toward the raft. The paddler in the boat farthest away from the unconscious person then reaches across his partner's kayak, grabs the victim's wrists, and with a concentrated heave pulls him over and across the raft. The patient is then turned over and mouth-to-mouth resuscitation can begin.

It is possible for the two-person raft to be

11-4. Raft-assisted mouth-to-mouth resuscitation on the water

towed to shore by a third paddler, but in populated areas it would be far more prudent to send up a distress rocket the moment the unconscious person is sighted. In this way, professional help can be on its way while mouth-to-mouth resuscitation is in progress. Remember that anyone who has been unconscious for any reason should be examined by a doctor as soon as possible.

Kayak-Supported Resuscitation

To perform resuscitation in the water while supported by a kayak (fig. 11-5) you must first jump out of your boat. Be careful not to capsize it and do not forget to put your paddle in the paddle park. Hold onto the front of your kayak by its lifting toggle. Using this as a support, bend the patient's head well back over your arm. Make sure you keep your hand off his throat and start mouth-to-mouth resuscitation. It is not easy and you will find it awkward and exhausting work.

Shock

How bad the shock is depends on the severity of its cause. Shock usually accompanies injuries, sudden illness, or severe pain.

11-5. Kayak-supported mouth-to-mouth resuscitation in the water

Shock may be recognized by one or more of the following:

- Your companion may look very white-faced.
- His pulse rate becomes faster but weaker.
- He will start to pant with quick, rapid breaths.
- He is sweating but his skin is cold and clammy.
- He may feel sick and vomit.
- He may become very anxious.
- He could complain of thirst.
- He may feel faint and dizzy and complain of blurred vision.

To treat shock you should first of all try to deal with whatever has caused the shock. Then lay the patient down, head low and turned to one side. Raise the legs if possible and loosen all clothing at the neck, chest, and waist. Cover him with a sleeping bag or blanket and reassure him continually. You could moisten his lips with water if he complains of thirst.

Do not heat the victim with hot water bottles or anything else that could drain heat from the inner vital organs.

Do not give the victim anything to drink, and if he is injured, keep him still.

Hypothermia

Hypothermia is the main killer of water users and those who seek recreation out of doors. It is caused by exposure to cold and is aggravated by wet, exhaustion, and wind. To die of cold it is not necessary to be in arctic conditions; most cases occur in temperatures between 30 and 50 degrees Fahrenheit.

There are many situations that can cause people to become dangerously cold, but there are some that are specific to paddlers. Immersion in cold water is the obvious cause, but the not-so-obvious danger is when a person is being towed. If the kayaker has been paddling hard before needing assistance, his body will be soaked with perspiration, and the sudden inactivity will make him vulnerable to the chilling effect of the wind. Once on land, pitching a tent in wind and driving rain when soaked with perspiration is also dangerous.

If you are a leader, think in terms of hypothermia all the time, and remember that just because you feel fine does not mean that your group feels the same. Be aware of the condition of others and the moment you think all is not well, paddle for land, make camp, and light a roaring fire. Disregard people who say they feel fine when their symptoms tell you otherwise.

Cold kills in two stages. The first stage is exposure and exhaustion. The minute you start to lose body heat faster than your body produces it, you are suffering from exposure. To remedy this, you can flap your arms about and jump up and down. Meanwhile, your internal heating system makes involuntary adjustments to preserve the heat to the inner core of vital organs—you shiver. Unfortunately, this will drain your reserves of energy. The only way to stop this drain is to get some distance away from the cause of your discomfort, put on some dry clothing, and drink something hot.

The second stage is hypothermia. If you are unable to escape from the conditions that are chilling you, your condition will deteriorate until your energy reserves are exhausted and cold starts to affect the brain. At this stage people start to act irrationally and gibber nonsense incessantly. They do not answer questions put to them. This is because the brain has been cooled to such an extent that they lose the power to act and think sensibly. They are now beyond caring and are unable to help themselves. The internal temperature is now dropping fast. Consciousness will come and go. If the condition is not treated, the sufferer will soon lapse into a coma, then very quickly collapse completely and die.

A review of the symptoms and accompanying body temperature is as follows:

- Uncontrollable shivering (91 to 98 degrees Fahrenheit).
- Shivering stops, muscles become rigid, speech is slurred, erratic paddling (90 to 91 degrees Fahrenheit).
- Lapses in memory, incoherent speech, paddling stops. If on land, stumbling and drowsiness. To sleep is to die (83 to 88 degrees Fahrenheit).
- Complete exhaustion, unconsciousness (83 degrees Fahrenheit).
- Death (77 degrees Fahrenheit).

Treatment for Hypothermia

The treatment for hypothermia will depend on what facilities are at hand. If the patient is only semiconscious, you will need medical help immediately, but while you are waiting, here is what you need to do:

- Get the patient out of the cold and into warm shelter.
- Put him into a polyethylene exposure bag while others look for a house, erect a tent, build a shelter, dig a snow hole, or otherwise secure shelter. If you are alone with the victim, you may have to decide whether to continue warming the patient or to leave him in the hope of getting help quickly. The important consideration is just how bad the patient's condition is. If he is very bad, it is better to stay and do all you can. Unfortunately, this is something of a *Catch-22* situation.
- Handle the patient carefully. Carry him with the head lower than the feet. His blood pressure will be low and this will keep the blood circulating to the brain.
- Once out of the wind, gently take his clothes off. Do not massage him.
- If breathing is very shallow or the patient has difficulty breathing, you can assist him with mouth-to-mouth resuscitation. If possible, warm air should be administered by exhaling into a face mask worn by the patient.
- Start to rewarm the patient using one of the following methods. If you have been lucky enough to find a house with a bath, place the victim into stirred hot water 105 to 112 degrees Fahrenheit—test it with your elbow. Support his legs and arms so they are out of the water. If you heat the limbs, the cold blood will change places with the warm blood from the inner core, causing further cooling at the vital organs. If you do not have access to a bath, apply hot towels or blankets (115 degrees Fahrenheit) to the patient's chest, neck, groin, and abdomen. Remember, do not attempt to heat his arms and legs. If you have not found a shelter, get the patient into an exposure bag or tent. Once out of the wind, take his clothes off gently and put him into a sleeping bag. Then get some fit warm person to undress and

get into the bag with him. Bear in mind that this is no time for prudery—a life is at stake.

Once the patient starts to perspire, recovery is rapid, usually taking one to two hours. At no time during the treatment should alcohol be given to the patient because this will cause the hot/cold blood exchange between the surface and the inner core mentioned earlier. At any time after the patient becomes semiconscious, however, hot, sweet drinks can be given. They will do little to heat the inner core, but will work wonders with the patient's morale.

Survival Time in Cold Water

The survival time of a poorly clothed person in cold water varies according to a number of factors and different circumstances, but the numbers in figure 11-6 can be taken as a general rule.

Survival and the Inner Person

Strange things happen when things go wrong. At the moment of fear or stress, a phase of mental and physical activity is triggered off and the body is alerted by a sudden release of adrenaline. Blood pressure and heart rate increase and the liver sends an increased amount of sugar into the bloodstream. The blood vessels to the skin are restricted, allowing more blood to go to the muscles, which makes them more easily stimulated

Water Surface Temperature		Time of Immersion for Survival
Centigrade	Fahrenheit	
0	32	15 minutes or less.
2.5	36.5	30 minutes.
5	41	1 hour.
10	50	3 hours.
15	59	7 hours.

11-6. *Survival times in cold water*

and less easily tired. Heat loss is reduced and mental activity is increased. Put all these factors together and you have the formula for either survival or panic.

How people feel within themselves has a great deal to do with their ability to survive. People who think they are beaten usually are. It is the will to survive, that indomitable spirit deep within, that helps humans to conquer. To some, fear brings unexpected strength. Others become so weak that gripping a paddle shaft is more than they can manage. Anxiety, doubt, fear, apprehension, and despair are all nails in the coffin of survival. But knowledge dispels fear, and practice in realistic but controlled conditions makes an accident less to be feared when it happens.

Calling a Halt to a Trip

Kayak trips may last a couple of days or several weeks, but illness and injuries do not respect people and their plans. It may be necessary at some stage of a trip to call the whole thing off and seek assistance. To help make that decision, the time is right to call a halt if any members of the group complain of the following symptoms:
- Any bleeding that will not stop
- Any diarrhea that will not stop
- Vomiting that does not respond to treatment
- Severe chest pains that are persistent
- Any kind of paralysis
- A persistent fever
- Severe and persistent stomach pains
- Shortness of breath or difficulty in breathing
- Inability to pass urine
- Any persistent disturbance of speech or vision or any mental disorder
- A serious bite or sting—for example, scorpion, spider, or poisonous snake
- Any blow to the head that has caused a loss of consciousness

STRATEGIES FOR SURVIVAL

During any expedition along wild and unpopulated coastlines it must be accepted that at some stage it may be necessary, due to injury or illness, to abort the trip. You may have to leave kayaks behind and make a journey over inhospitable country in order to save yourself or to get help for others. Group leaders should make sure that anyone they send to get help is fully equipped and has adequate food and water packed.

The following hints are included to prepare the kayaker for some emergency situations.

Water and Thirst

Water that has been filtered through rocks or comes from deep springs is usually fit to drink, but beware of slow-moving streams; no matter how fresh the water looks, the rotting body of a fox or other animal may be lying in the water only a few hundred yards upstream from where you are drinking.

If there is any doubt about the purity of water, treat it with water purification tablets, use about five drops of domestic bleach to a pint of water, or just boil it.

If you have to leave your kayak and travel across hot desert country, it is always best to travel at night when it is cool. In that way you lose far less moisture from your body. If you must walk under the hot sun, keep your body covered and your sleeves down, so your body fluids will be retained longer. Do not walk any distance in hot weather while wearing a wet suit; people have been known to collapse and die from heat exhaustion doing just that. It is never a good idea to ration water. You will last longer if you drink your fill rather than taking small sips over a long period.

Remember, even in cold conditions paddling a kayak a long way fast can cause you to perspire excessively, which in turn can cause your body to dehydrate. Therefore, regulate your paddling speed over long distances.

Drinking melted snow without boiling it first can cause diarrhea. Pack ice is composed of salt water, but any floating ice that has come from a glacier was once snow, so it should be fresh water—even if the snow did fall at the time of the Crusades!

Salt Water

You can cook in it, boil in it, wash in it, or swim in it, but never drink it. The presence of salt

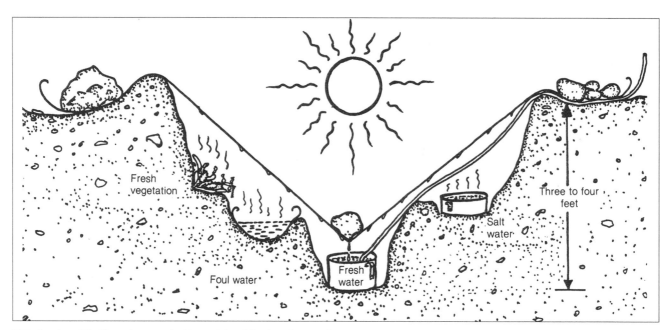

12-1. A solar still will produce one to three pints of fresh water per day.

water, however, can often help you to find fresh water in a place you would never think of looking.

When the tide is at its lowest, locate the high-water mark and dig a few holes on either side of it. You may come to water, and because fresh water is lighter than salt water, it will float to the top. There might only be a thin layer, so suck it out with some tubing or a piece of hollow grass. It might even be possible to rig something up to the kayak's bilge pump, although I have not tried this. The water you extract will be rather murky, but it is not salty and will certainly be better than nothing.

The Solar Still

The solar still produces fresh water. Dig a hole and line it with a clear polyethylene sheet (fig. 12-1). Any foul water may be placed in hollows lined with smaller pieces of polyethylene. The sun evaporates the foul water and the moisture from the fresh vegetation. This condenses when it

touches the clean plastic sheet, and the droplets run down into the container at the bottom. Use a tube to retrieve the fresh water, because if you move the sheeting, the whole process will have to start again.

Fire

The importance of a fire cannot be overestimated. It is not just a means of cooking, it is the focal point of any campsite. It is a social center where clothes and equipment can be dried, cold bodies warmed, and chilled spirits raised. Things never appear so desperate if discussed around the hot, bright flame of a wood fire.

When you are attempting to light a fire, there is no point in trying to be a purist. Carry tablets to light the fire with you, well sealed and away from your food. Carry both ordinary and windproof/waterproof matches. Spread them around into different packs so that no matter how wet things get, there will always be some dry matches somewhere. If you do not carry fire lighters, keep a good supply of kindling with you, such as dried moss, charred cloth, or the thin paperlike surface of birch bark, which burns well even when wet. Keep fires away and downwind from tents.

Lighting a Fire by Friction

Lighting a fire without a match is a soul-destroying job, but you never know just how badly a fire may be needed. Of all the methods I have seen demonstrated, the following North American Indian method is the best (see fig. 12-2).

Place the fireboard, as shown in the figure, with the notch on the tinder. Kneel and steady the fireboard with your foot. Hold the spindle, revolving it with long strokes. Keep increasing the pressure. Do not give up until the smoke rises. Blow gently, then knock the hot ember that has been formed into the tinder. Blow steadily but gently until a flame begins, then lay some dry, tiny, previously prepared twigs. If ever a skill needed perseverance, this is it. It does work, but it needs practice. The Eskimos used a specially shaped mouthpiece to hold the spindle. Although I have never tried this, it is probably easier and it leaves one hand free to feed the moss or tinder onto the hot ember.

12-2. This illustration shows how to light a fire by friction. Tools for starting a fire by friction consist of: an octagonal spindle approximately 1 foot long and ¾ inch thick (A); a fireboard approximately 4 inches wide, ½ inch thick, and 1 foot long with hollows and V-shaped cuts for the spindle (B); a wooden handpiece to rest on top of the spindle (C); a bow approximately 2 feet long with a leather thong or bootlace (D); and extra tinder (moss, shredded bark, wood shavings) to be drying out for the next fire (E).

Lighting a Fire with a Camera Lens

In bright sunlight, it is possible to light a fire using a camera lens. The wider you can open the lens the more heat will be produced. Open the back of the camera and hold its open back toward the sun. Focus the sunlight so that it appears on the kindling material—moss or cotton wool—as a bright, white point of light. Get a red ember and blow gently but steadily; then lay the kindling on some predried tiny twigs.

With some kinds of eyeglasses (those from a far-sighted person) it is possible to concentrate enough heat to start a flame, but the sunlight must focus to a point to generate enough heat.

Flint and Steel

Speaking as someone who used to enjoy blasting off flintlock firearms (for years I had only one eyebrow!), I can vouch for the efficiency of the spark that is generated when flint and steel are struck together. To light a fire then, you can use a piece of flint and any piece of steel to strike against it. Using your best knife will not extend its life expectancy, so use an old blunt one.

Place your dry tinder around a piece of moss or cotton wool that has been doused with a few drops of lighter fluid. Strike your piece of flint a glancing blow with the steel, directing your spark onto the cotton wool. If the spark is well aimed, the cotton wool and the tinder will burst into flame.

Flint strikers can be bought from most outdoor stores and come in two parts, the striker and the steel. The striker is made from a mixture of flint and iron filings. To make a spark, the striker is forced quickly across a preshaped piece of serrated steel, which is usually attached to the striker itself. One of these strikers is well worth a permanent place in your repair kit.

Carbide Pellets

Carry some carbide pellets in aluminum foil or an empty film container. To light your fire, place some pellets on dry tinder. Allow some of your saliva to dribble onto the carbide. As soon as the liquid touches the pellets and the carbide starts to fizz, light the highly inflammable acetylene gas that is given off. Now is the time to use your match or spark to ignite the gas and the tinder.

A word of caution: Do not carry your carbide in any tightly sealed screw-top container. As a kayaker, you should know by now that some moisture can *always* find its way into a "watertight" container. As small boys, my pals and I used to place pieces of carbide into a can, spit on the lumps, quickly jam the lid on, and place stones on top of the can. We would then run for it. The minor explosion that followed would send the rocks flying high into the air. We soon discovered that the tighter the container the bigger the explosion.

Snares

When you carry wire and twine in your repair kit and there is small game about, you will always have the means of filling the cooking pot. Setting snares can take some ingenuity, but the accompanying illustration (fig. 12-3) gives some ideas.

12-3. Methods of setting snares

It is a gallant business, this kaiak-hunting; it is like a sportive dance with the sea and with death. There is no finer sight possible than to see the kaiak-man breasting the heavy rollers that seem utterly to engulf him. Or when, overtaken by a storm at sea, the kaiaks run for the shore, they come like black storm-birds rushing before the wind and the waves, which, like rolling mountains, sweep on in their wake. The paddles whirl through the air and water, the body is bent a little forwards, the head often turned half backwards to watch the seas; all is life and spirit—while the sea around reeks like a seething cauldron. And then it may happen that when the game is at its wildest a seal pops its head up before them. Quicker than thought the harpoon is seized and rushes through the foam with deadly aim; the seal dashes away with the bladder behind it, but is presently caught and killed, and then towed onwards. Everything is done with the same masterly skill and with the same quiet demeanour. The Eskimo never dreams that he is performing feats of heroism. (Nansen, Eskimo Life, p. 58.)

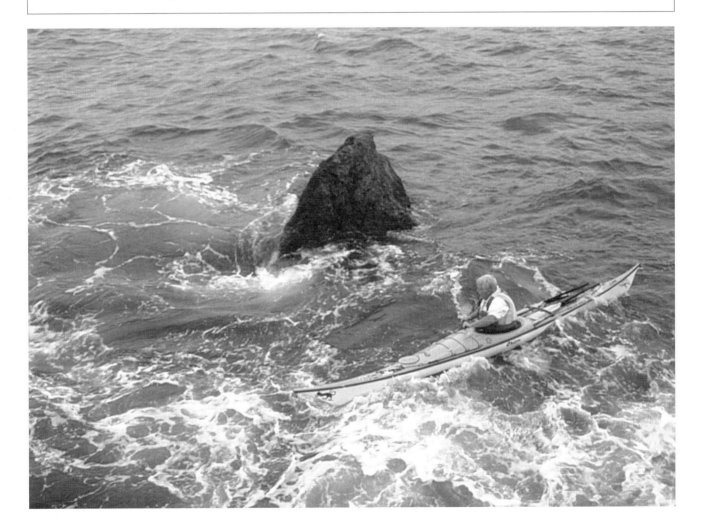

First find some tracks or flattened grass that will indicate an animal run. Make an easy running loop in the wire. Then, when the snare is set, make sure that the bottom of the loop is not less than a palm's width from the ground.

Fishing

Under normal circumstances, fishing is one of the easiest ways of obtaining a meal when you are out in a coastal wilderness. There are numerous ways of going about this.

Trolling

Trolling is an ideal method for the kayak paddler. A line is towed behind the boat under the water at a speed of about 3 miles per hour. Any faster than this and the sinker will plane to the surface together with the hook, defeating the whole object of the exercise. A trolling rig for mackerel and pollack is illustrated in figure 12-4. The depth of the line behind the kayak is governed by the weight of the lead.

12-4. A trolling rig for mackerel and pollack

Overnight Line

Leaving a line out at night (fig. 12-5) may be the lazy man's way, but there is nothing like having the line work for you while you are asleep. Stretch the line out between two trees or boulders or just anchor it with pegs. Hang as many traces from it as you like. Floats can be made from small pieces of driftwood. Allow for the movement of the tide so that any fish caught are not left high and dry during the night.

Jigging

The paternoster trace is ideal for jigging up and down (fig. 12-6). This is an excellent method of catching many different types of fish, especially mackerel. About six traces can be fastened to one line. Any more than this and the whole setup becomes downright dangerous if you fill all the hooks at the same time, which is not difficult when the mackerel are running. Feathers or plastic eels can be used as a lure, and the line is moved slowly up and down while the kayak is stationary.

Gaffing

If the area you visit has an abundance of salmon streams, you may find that gaffing is an easy way to fill your cooking pot. You can improvise a

12-5. An overnight line

12-6. *The paternoster trace*

12-7. *Fishing implements made from scissors, a folding knife, or wood*

gaff by using scissors, a folding knife, or wood (see fig. 12-7). Next, find a salmon stream. Look for a shallow place, either at the mouth or below rapids, and hook the salmon out as they fight their way upstream. Gaffing is not the sportsman's way of catching salmon, but that is hardly a valid consideration when your stomach is empty. You can always apologize to the salmon as it is baking in foil!

A word of warning: If, when you arrive at your chosen fishing spot, there are a lot of half-chewed salmon lying about and you are in bear country, be on your guard or go somewhere else.

Making Nets and Hooks

Small hand-fishing nets can be made from string vests or mosquito netting. Fishhooks can be adapted from old fish bones, safety pins, or sail needles softened in a fire and bent to shape.

Gathering Food from the Shoreline

If you do not have much luck with your rod and line skills, do not give up. There are other ways of gaining sustenance from the sea—just go out and pick it up. The old Aleut saying, "When the tide is out the table is set," is as true now as it ever was. Having lived all my life by the seacoast, I grew up with children who ate whelks, mussels, and crabs the way others eat candy. Precautions must be taken, however, because most rock seafoods must be properly collected and prepared and eaten fresh. In most cases, the creatures are cooked while still alive.

One strong word of warning: Before kayaking in an area where you intend to eat inshore seafood, inquire to make sure that pollution from mercury or a red tide has not rendered the animals highly dangerous for human consumption.

Limpets

Limpets (fig. 12-8A) can be found on almost any seashore on rocks at low tide. The secret is to quickly pull them off the rocks before they have time to get a good grip.

The keyhole limpet (fig. 12-8B) is not a true limpet, but it looks like one because of its coolie hat shape and the muscular foot on the bottom. It is just as good to eat as a limpet, and it can be identified by the missing apex of the shell leaving an almost round hole. The shell is usually gray in color or has brown and white radiating ridges.

To prepare limpets, loosen them from the shell with a knife and cut off the foot portion. Limpets are tough, so put them between some muslin cloth and beat them with a piece of wood—or a meat mallet if you have one—to tenderize them. Limpets can be boiled or panfried alone or with batter. If you carry a portable mincer, you can mince the limpets to use in a chowder or to give body to a soup.

Whelks

Whelks (figs. 12-8C and D) are sea snails. They come in any number of varieties and are eaten throughout the world. They also come in a variety of colors and shapes. Some shells are smooth and some are wrinkled, and they vary in size from 1 to 2 inches. The opening at the bottom is closed by a hard trapdoor, which is attached to the edible foot of the animal.

To prepare, let the whelks soak for about three to four hours. Scrub the shells, cover them with water, and boil them gently for twenty minutes. Drain the water off and chill them. A pin will help you remove the snail from its shell. When you do this, the intestines will stay in the shell, so you can eat all you pull out. They can be dipped in melted butter or in a cocktail or tartar sauce if you have had room for such luxuries. You can also grind them up as you did the limpets.

Clams

The soft bodies of clams are enclosed, or partially so, by two shells, which can be tightly closed. The body of the razor clam (fig. 12-8E) is not completely enclosed by its smooth, brown, shiny shell. They are good to eat, but you will have to be fast to catch them because they can bury and hide themselves under the sand very quickly.

To prepare razor clams, place them in containers filled with salt water and allow them to clean themselves for several hours. Then run a sharp knife along each side of the shell to cut the muscle that holds the shell shut and allows it to open. If you intend to fry the whole clam, use a pair of scissors to cut through the next siphon. The dark-colored stuff near the hinge is the liver, which is nutritious and full of flavor.

The littleneck clam (fig. 12-8F) is also called the rock or butter clam and varies in color from gray or cream to a mottled brown or yellow. Shells grow to about 2 inches across.

To prepare littleneck clams, wash with a brush before steaming in a small amount of water. Once the shell has opened up, the clam may be served in melted butter.

Cockles

When looked at from the side, cockles appear heart-shaped (fig. 12-8G). They are to be found just under the surface in sand or mud.

To prepare cockles, leave them for several hours in a bucket of seawater in the shade so that they have time to clean themselves of all their mud and grit. Then boil as with other shellfish.

Scallops

Scallops (fig. 12-8H) are easily recognized by their fan-shaped shells, which seem to be collected

12-8. Edible shellfish

all over the world. Most scallops swim by opening and shutting their shells. They are found in shallow water.

To prepare scallops, slide a sharp knife between the shells and cut the holding muscle. The shells will then come apart easily. Cover the animal with bread crumbs and fry, or wrap in bacon and broil, or sauté in butter.

Oysters

Oysters (fig. 12-8I) have irregular-shaped shells, which are fluted in gray and white. They vary in shape, depending on the particular species—some tend to be elongated while others are more circular.

To prepare oysters, cut the hinge muscle as described for clams. Oysters can be eaten raw or dipped in batter made from a mixture of eggs and milk. They can then be rolled in whole wheat flour or cornmeal and fried for a couple of minutes in hot fat or oil.

Mussels

Mussels (fig. 12-8J) are found all over the world—I know because I always seem to be scratching my kayak on mussel beds! The shells are blue, black, or brown and grow in colonies on just about any solid object. When cooked, the animals turn an orange-brown. To reduce the risk of eating polluted mussels, eat only those that are exposed to the air for long periods of time. Be sure to inquire about the area in which you are gathering them. The livers of mussels collect harmful nitrates from the sea.

To prepare mussels, scrape the shells to remove the seaweed, barnacles, and the beards (sometimes known as "dead man's hair"—but don't let that put you off). Wash them thoroughly and put them into a steamer to open, then eat them after dipping them in hot butter or lemon sauce.

Chitons

Chitons (fig. 12-8K) are strange creatures that are to be found all over the world near the low tide mark. The smaller ones attach themselves to the undersides of small rocks. The giant chiton can be found crawling about on seaweed or rocks, near the low tide mark.

To prepare chitons, be sure to clean them immediately after they are gathered because they deteriorate rapidly. Pull the smooth foot off from the underneath, then scrape and wash. The Indians of the Pacific Coast used to eat them raw. If you prefer, chitons can be beaten into tenderness and fried with egg batter or crisp crumbs.

Octopus

You might find a small octopus (fig. 12-9) stranded by the tide or hiding in the crevices of a rocky pool. They live on small crustaceans and mollusks, so do not worry about finding the remains of one of the local divers in its stomach.

To prepare octopus, first remove the skin. This can be done by rubbing with a coarse salt. Keep

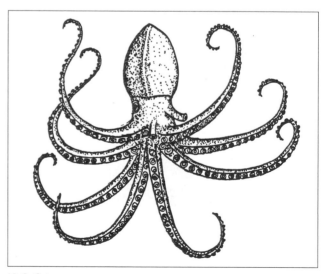

12-9. Octopus

rinsing well with water and continue rubbing until the skin tears off easily. The arms can be cut into thin slices and smoked, or the meat can be pounded until tender and fried in bread crumbs. Do not overfry octopus or it will get tough.

Sea Urchins

I once had three or four very large, spiny sea urchins (fig. 12-10) busily wandering and crackling about underneath my spray cover in the cockpit area of my kayak. It was at the end of a hot summer day and I was wearing a pair of swimming trunks and a T-shirt. I forgot all about them until I decided to treat myself to an Eskimo roll to cool off. It was only when I had my head upside down in the water that I was reminded that I was not alone in the cockpit. I probably executed the fastest roll on record. Earlier that day, I watched in horror while one of the lighthouse keepers on Northumberland's Longstone Lighthouse picked up a sea urchin. He proceeded to stick his fingers inside, scoop out the eggs, and eat them raw. He assured me afterwards that these were a great delicacy. In a kayak it is an easy matter to collect sea urchins. You will see them clinging to rocks just below the surface as you paddle along. Kill them only if you are going to eat them. It is surely wrong to kill a living creature just because it is beautiful or interesting to look at.

To prepare sea urchins, you can boil them in their shells and then split open the shells to obtain the meat. Many people, like the lighthouse keeper, consider the eggs a delicacy. If you wish, however, the eggs can be washed out with the rest of the internal organs. In Australia live sea urchins are thrown into an open fire to burn off the spines. The shells are then opened and the insides eaten while still hot.

Barnacles

Barnacles (fig. 12-11) are to be found all over the world, and all the types are edible. The gooseneck barnacle is usually found in rocky crevices in areas where there is big surf. Ships also have barnacles, and you might even prize one from the back of a friendly whale.

To prepare barnacles, cook them as soon as possible after collection. Wash carefully in fresh water, then put a little water in the bottom of a steamer pan. As soon as the water starts to boil, put the barnacles in the top of the pan. When they can be handled, remove the top part and the rough skin. The meat is red and resembles that of a crab, but it has more flavor.

Shrimp

You will find shrimp (fig. 12-12) in rock pools at low tide. To prepare, drop them into a pan of boiling salted water and let them boil for fifteen to

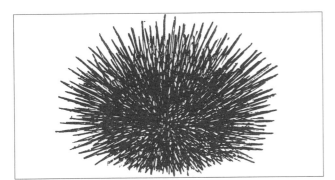

12-10. Giant red sea urchin

12-11. Barnacles

12-12. Shrimp

twenty minutes. Then pour off the hot water and cool them in cold water. Hold the body tightly, then break off the head and peel away the thin shell. The shrimp can then be eaten as part of a salad or fried in batter.

Crabs and Lobsters

Because crabs and lobsters are more common than some of the other sea creatures I have discussed, I will not go into detail about how to catch them. Traps are usually required, though you may be fortunate enough to find them in tide pools or shallow water. Crabs and lobsters should be dropped live into boiling salted water and cooked for twenty minutes.

Some Simple Ropework

If you happen to be a climber as well as a kayaker—and many people seem to be able to combine these activities quite well—then by all means carry the special equipment with you inside your boat. The advice I give here is for the non-

climber who just happens to find herself in an awkward position, but who has had the presence of mind to carry a length of rope as part of her equipment.

Finding yourself stormbound on some tiny beach is not so rare as you may think. If the beach is on a headland or promontory, there may be calm water quite close at hand, but you may be separated from it by steep rocks and cliffs. This will mean a strenuous portage. A knowledge of simple ropework may save injury to yourself and prevent your equipment from bouncing down a cliff. Knowing how to lower yourself and your kayak is also important. On the other hand, if you take part in some careless glacier walking, you could finish up down a crevasse and if you cannot climb a rope, you might not get out again.

Abseiling

Lowering yourself down a cliff on a rope is not so difficult if you know how. In the method known as the classic abseil or rappel (fig. 12-13) the rope is doubled around an anchor, or belay point, so that both halves of the rope hang down.

To perform this maneuver, walk slowly backward down the slope or face, keeping your legs at right angles to it if possible. The speed of your descent is adjusted by the angle of the rope held in the right hand. The rope should be held firmly but not tightly in the left hand. With the rope around your right thigh and left shoulder, lean back and let the strain be taken on those areas. The right leg should be kept lower than the left, with the rope well up under your behind. Remember to lower yourself slowly to avoid bad friction burns that could make paddling your kayak very uncomfortable.

Long descents by this method can be very painful, but it is ideal for drops of 15 to 20 feet or for slowly keeping pace with a kayak that is also making its way down a cliff.

12-13. *The classic abseil, or rappel, is a good method of lowering yourself down a cliff.*

12-14. *Lowering a kayak down a cliff*

Lowering a Kayak

In figure 12-14, the person could quite easily make a couple of turns around the tree with the rope and lower the kayak in that fashion. If the ledge is narrow, the paddler must belay (secure) himself around a rock or to a peg hammered into the rock.

Climbing a Rope

No matter how strong you are, if you are frightened, the rope is thin, and your hands are cold, you are certainly not going to climb it. Unfortunately, you may have fallen into a crevasse, and you cannot stay there forever.

You will need three separated loops of rope dropped down to you. These can be taken from the towlines of the kayaks, but make sure that the loops are thinner than the rope you intend to climb. Your ascent is made possible by what is known as a Prusik knot (fig. 12-15). This knot can

be pushed up or along a rope quite easily when there is no tension on the loop; but the moment any sudden pressure is put on it, the loop will grip fast to the main rope (figs. 12-15A and B).

This method of climbing with Prusik knots takes some practice, but it is easily mastered (fig. 12-15C). First take the weight off one foot and slide up the knot on that side as high as it will go. Then put your weight back on the higher foot, take it off the lower foot, and slide the lower knot as high as it will go. Next take the weight of your body on both feet and slide up the knot from the chest rope as high as you can. Continue in this manner until the rope is climbed. This is a slow method of gaining height, but it is reliable and foolproof so long as the rope and anchor point are strong.

Glaciers

Many glaciers eventually find their way to the sea, and to paddle near to them is an unforgettable experience. As you paddle closer to the base of a glacier, the danger increases. At any time huge

12-15. *Climbing a rope with the use of a Prusik knot*

quantities of ice can fall from the face with a thunderous roar, creating quite alarming tidal waves.

Glacial ice exhibits the most beautiful shades of blues and greens, and the temptation to wander across this turquoise wonderland is a real one.

If you feel that a glacier might lie on your route, you are well advised to carry certain items of equipment: at least one length of good climbing rope, an ice ax, and a pair of crampons for each person.

Crampons

Crampons are strapped to your boots to prevent you from slipping on ice. They have ten or twelve sharp points that bite into the snow or ice and enable you to walk safely. The twelve-pointed crampons are probably the best to use because they have two forward points that can be kicked straight into a steep ice slope. Crampons must fit the boots tightly. Slack crampons will feel insecure and are dangerous, especially when walking sideways (traversing) across a slope. When you are traversing, place your feet flat to the ice slope. Make sure that all the points are in contact with the ice face. Keep the crampon points protected when not in use.

Ice Ax

The best ice ax for general use is the traditional type with a long shaft. When held by the head, the shaft should be long enough for the end to touch the ground (making the ice ax ideal for using as a walking stick). Ice axes have a wide adze blade on one side of the head for cutting steps in snow and, on the other side, a sharp spike for cutting into hard ice. At the end of the ax there is a pointed ferrule, handy to use as a probe to test the depth of the snow. All ice axes should be fitted with a sling.

When walking on ice, hold the ice ax like a walking stick, with the sling around your wrist and the adze toward you. If you hold the ax like this, getting into the correct position to stop a slide will be almost automatic. The second you feel yourself falling, roll onto your front and force the point into the snow, the head of the ax level with your shoulder (fig. 12-16A). The shaft should slope down across your body to the opposite side. Hold the shaft three-quarters of the way down with the left hand. To help dig the point in deep, lever from the elbow.

Do not stick the point into the ice too hard or too suddenly. Otherwise the ax might be snatched out of your hand. As you slide, try to exert an even pressure. On very steep slopes, the friction can be increased by lifting your body clear at the thighs so your knees press into the snow (fig. 12-

12-16. The ice ax self-arrest

12-17. If your tent is lost or destroyed, you can build a shelter in the snow.

16B). If you are wearing crampons, you must keep them clear of the face in this manner because they can dig in and cause you to somersault and lose control. This happened to one of my friends and he was skewered through the ribs on his own ice ax. Luckily, he survived.

Snow Hole

I can remember a number of unfortunate things that have happened to tents on some of my trips. One tent was half-eaten by pack rats on the Aleutian Islands, and another was completely burnt out on a Scottish island. If your tent is lost or destroyed, and the ground is deep with snow, there is certainly no need to freeze to death—just build a snow hole or a snowhouse. There are two points to remember, however. First, construct your sleeping area well above ground level (fig. 12-17)—you will be warmer the higher up you are. Second, remember to leave a ventilation hole so you do not suffocate.

Getting Help

The following methods are not listed in any particular order of priority; your EPIRB (see p. 148) should be the *last* option, however. There are numerous ways to signal for assistance.

- Fire a gun at intervals of one minute—but do not blast off all your ammunition if you think there is no one to hear.
- Sound your fog horn continually.
- Set off any red flare, parachute flare, dye-marker, or orange smoke.
- Spell out SOS in sand or snow or flash Morse code with a torch or mirror.

- Repeat "mayday" on your VHF transceiver (see below).
- Slowly raise and lower your arms.
- Wave a paddle slowly from side to side above your head.
- Send someone paddling off to get help.
- Set three fires in a triangle—this is accepted by pilots as a distress signal.
- Blow blasts on a whistle in groups of six.
- Make a smoky fire with leaves or rags.
- Fly a parafoil kite above tree level. They are easy to see and could also carry up a radio antenna.
- Activate your EPIRB.

Emergency Position Indicating Radio Beacon (EPIRB)

To activate an EPIRB you merely pull out the pin. Once you have done this, the device gives off a continual electronic bleep on the International Aviation Distress Frequency. This signal will be picked up by one of the Search and Rescue (SAR) satellites that circle the earth. The signal is then bounced back down to earth again, where it is picked up by a Local User Terminal (LUT) or Mission Control Center (MCC). Once activated, this signal will continue automatically for twenty-four to thirty-six hours and will indicate your position to the rescue services within a radius of 4.5 miles.

I must stress that pulling the pin on a radio beacon is your *last* option and should be considered only in the event of a *life-threatening situation,* after all the other rescues explained in this book have been attempted. Remember that you have the means of calling upon rescue services worldwide; the ultimate cost of any frivolous or unnecessary rescue attempt could be enormous. Because of the appalling high false-alarm rate, the signal from your EPIRB will not be acted upon until confirmed by the SAR satellite on its second orbit.

VHF Radio (Transceiver)

There is nothing like a friendly voice—indeed any voice—to comfort you when you're in trouble. When you shoot a parachute flare into the sky, you will always wonder if you are the only person in the world who is watching it float down. With the VHF radio you do not have this uncertainty, because, if your batteries are fully charged, you should soon find yourself in voice contact with a human being on the other end of the line.

At sea level your signal has a range of 5 to 10 miles. The greater your elevation, the farther your signal will travel. Your "Mayday . . . Mayday . . . Mayday" call will be transmitted on Channel 16, which is the International Distress Channel and is constantly monitored. Remember to give your position when you receive a reply. If you are out of range of a Search and Rescue (SAR) center, your distress call can be picked up by any fishing boat or other vessel and then relayed to a SAR center.

Modern sets are waterproof and small enough to be held in the hand. This means they can be kept nearby and can even be carried in a life-jacket pocket. If you neglect to maintain the batteries in your VHF set, you may well have to revert to scratching your SOS in the sand with a stick.

Signaling with Mirrors

Signaling with mirrors is one of the most effective ways of attracting attention, so it is well worth making an effort to master the skills involved. The reflection of sunlight in a small mirror can be seen for many miles and so would be readily seen by a potential rescuer if he is looking your way, and if you can aim the direction of the mirror flash. While the former is up to providence, you can definitely do something about the latter.

To make sure your flashes get somewhere near the target, you need a special two-sided mir-

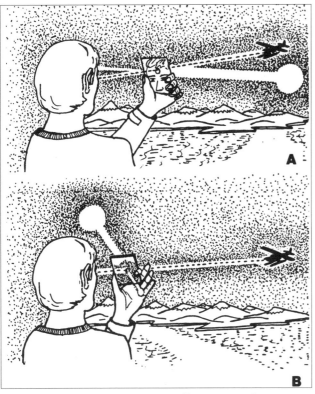

12-18. Signaling with mirrors is an effective way of attracting attention.

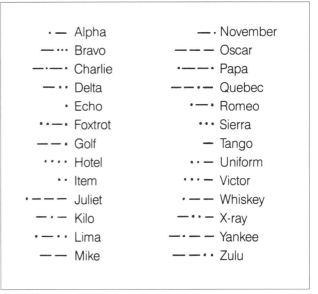

• —	Alpha	— •	November
— • • •	Bravo	— — —	Oscar
— • — •	Charlie	• — — •	Papa
— • •	Delta	— — • —	Quebec
•	Echo	• — •	Romeo
• • — •	Foxtrot	• • •	Sierra
— — •	Golf	—	Tango
• • • •	Hotel	• • —	Uniform
• •	Item	• • • —	Victor
• — — —	Juliet	• — —	Whiskey
— • —	Kilo	— • • —	X-ray
• — • •	Lima	— • — —	Yankee
— —	Mike	— — • •	Zulu

12-19. Morse code with phonetic alphabet

ror with a small hole in the middle. These signaling mirrors can be obtained at outdoor equipment stores or surplus stores. To signal your rescuer, first hold the mirror at arm's length and sight the plane (or whatever) through the small hole. If the plane is somewhere near the same position as the sun, move the mirrored side that faces you until you can see the sunlight spot coming through the hole and shining on your face. Keep moving the mirror until this spot of sunlight coincides with the hole in the center. The spot will appear to vanish into the hole in the center and, if the plane is still in the center of this hole, it will get a flashing reflection from your mirror (fig. 12-18A).

The sun, unfortunately, may not be near the object of your signaling. If the sun is well to the side and is more than a right angle from the target,

hold the mirror so that it shines through the center hole and falls on the palm of your hand (fig. 12-18B). Line up this little circle of brightness as seen in the mirror so that its reflection vanishes through the center hole of the mirror in the same way as when the sun fell on your face.

If this all sounds too complicated, and well it might, there is a simpler way although it is not as accurate. Hold your thumb up at arm's length. Sight your thumb under the target and flash the sun's reflection along your arm and off your thumb up onto the target. Try this first on a nearby tree or rock.

Morse Code and Semaphore

I certainly do not expect the kayak paddlers who read this book to rush immediately to learn by heart either the Morse code (fig. 12-19) or the system of relaying messages by semaphore (fig. 12-20). There may be a number of occasions, however, when both could be very useful; perhaps a

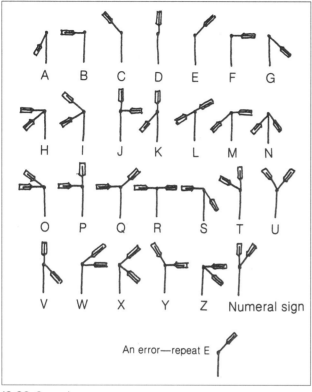

12-20. *Semaphore*

group becomes separated but are within sight of one another across the stormy waters between two islands. It would certainly be quite easy to pass messages by semaphore.

I would suggest, therefore, that both the Morse code and semaphore be inscribed or scratched somewhere—for instance on the inside of a hatch cover.

CAMPING

Let's Take the Tent

I was just about to pack the tent into my kayak, when an inner voice urged, "Hey man, this is Baja. You won't need a tent—it doesn't rain!" Despite feeling like an inadequate weakling—most of my kayaking companions were not bringing tents—I furtively smuggled the tent into my kayak. I was glad I did. I soon discovered that it doesn't have to rain for you to need a tent. You need some kind of barrier between you and those other little creatures who also feel chilly during the hours of darkness and who insist upon sharing the underside of your sleeping bag or the inside of your boots.

Because of violent daytime winds in Baja, the only practical times to make progress on the water was between 6:00 and 10:00 A.M. That meant I needed to get up and pack in pitch darkness around 4:00 A.M. I remember reading somewhere that flowers can grow in deserts because the dews are so heavy. I think I could have floated my kayak on the dew that had fallen during that first, tentless night.

When I finally emerged from my sopping wet bag of pulp, I had to feel around for the few pieces of clothing I had managed to keep dry next to my body during the night. By groping further, I managed to locate all those items of equipment that I had casually tossed down the previous evening. My last task was to force the sodden, sand-impregnated sleeping bag into its now wet, "waterproof" sack.

Later on during this trip, and contrary to prediction, it actually did rain. We had camped in an *arroyo* (a dry river bed). I learned afterwards that this is not one of the best places to pitch camp because rains in distant mountains can cause a flash flood. Some large, unpleasant, grey clouds appeared to materialize from nowhere, and I decided to pitch my tent.

The rain, when it arrived, was the horizontal sort that swirls from all sides and drenches everything. The direction and force of it made any attempt at a bivouac absolutely useless. I stayed dry in my tent, but there were a number of unhappy people that night. Luckily no wall of water came charging down the river bed to engulf us.

My advice is that if you are going to make an overnight stop and you have a tent, pack it in the boat. You never know what problems may arise, and it is comforting to have shelter at hand if you need it. If you really do have this constant urge to sleep under the stars, buy a tent with an inner roof zipper that opens up to reveal a mesh roof panel.

13-1. A place to pitch your tent can often be difficult to find. (Photo courtesy Barry Howell)

Tent Materials

Cotton

Cotton tents are still very popular although they tend to be heavier than man-made fibers. Cotton fabric breathes, allowing air to filter through the fine weave and thus giving you hardly any condensation. The trouble with cotton is that it will absorb water during heavy rain. It should therefore always be protected from water when stowed in your kayak. A wet cotton tent is much heavier than a dry one. In wet weather, these tents need a fly sheet. Cotton tents usually have to be folded carefully before they are packed away inside your kayak.

Waterproof Nylon

These tents do not need a fly sheet. They are quick to assemble and take up very little storage space. Their disadvantage is that although you will get no rain inside, they are like sauna baths even in dry, cool weather, and mopping out the condensation that collects inside can be a full-time job. After shaking off the water these tents can be stuffed straight into their storage bags without folding.

Waterproof Fly Sheet— Breathable Interior

These tents are very popular. The fly sheet can be left off in hot weather. In cool or rainy conditions, with proper ventilation and as long as the breathable material does not touch the exterior fly sheet, there is no condensation problem. These tents also pack away quickly. Although it is as well to fold the cotton inner tent, the waterproof fly sheet can be stuffed straight into its bag.

Regardless of the fabric you select, your tent should have panels that zip open in hot weather to reveal ventilating panels of mosquito netting.

What Size Tent?

After sitting in the cockpit of a kayak all day, it's nice to feel that you can stretch out in your own little kingdom. With the amount of storage space that a sea kayak has to offer, there is no need to skimp on the size of your tent. Live well and carry one suitable for two persons. This will not only give you room to sleep but give you sufficient space to thrash about and put on your paddling gear without subjecting your body to cramped contortions. Packing up is also easier because all your worldly possessions are within arm's reach.

During long rainy spells or when the local insects are thick and voraciously hungry, you will not feel so confined and you might even want to cook in the tent. This practice is not without its dangers, so if you must light a stove inside your tent always keep a *razor sharp* knife close at hand, that you can grab in a flash. Then if the tent material catches fire you cut your way out through the side of the tent. I have a memory of lying next to blackened, flapping rags, between two other shivering bodies, while the moon shone down on the remains of a tent that had been set on fire by the careless lighting of a gasoline stove. Fortunately, there had been no one in the tent at the time.

Try to choose a tent that has some kind of porch or vestibule. This is the safest place to cook in wet weather, and you have less chance of turning into a human torch. A vestibule also gives you a protected place in which to remove your dripping wet clothing during rain storms, and it will also house all that stinking wet paddling gear that we all know will not dry but do not want to get any wetter.

Basic Shapes and Types

Mountain Tents

These tents are the strongest and most weather resistant and are designed for use in hill country and on exposed windswept beaches. They are usually ridge shaped, with A poles at each end to support a ridge pole from which is slung the interior living compartment. A fly sheet reaches down to the ground all around, terminating in a wide skirt or snow valance. In high winds this valance

13-2. Chickee platform in the Everglades (Photo courtesy Linda Legg)

gives you something upon which to pile sand, stones, or driftwood. On the down side, these tents lack headroom and are usually cramped. By necessity their one entrance is usually small. They are, however, ideal for the serious expedition paddler who anticipates bad weather.

The pyramid mountain tent offers an alternative to the crouched camping position. The pyramid is formed by four interlocking aluminum poles. The inner compartment is slung from the apex of the connecting A poles, which means that it is possible to at least get off your knees while donning your wet suit. Like the mountain ridge, the fly sheet should touch the ground and should also have a snow valance. The entrance is usually small. Like the ridge, the pyramid will stand up to winds of storm force.

The strength of the mountain tent, whether ridge or pyramid design, is due to a canopy that is held and supported by stout aluminum tent poles. These poles are designed to neither flex nor bend. Once pitched, the tent is not freestanding but is meant to be pegged immovably to the ground.

Freestanding Tents

A very pleasant and functional tent for the everyday touring paddler is the kind that relies on thin, curved, flexible poles of either fiberglass or aluminum. The poles pass through sleeves or snap hooks fixed to the outside of a breathable ventilated inner tent. The poles are then bent and sprung into canvas sleeves sewn into the extremities of the sewn-in ground sheet. In wet weather, the inner tent is covered by a fly sheet. This type of construction enables the body of the tent to have convex walls, thus giving much more interior space for changing and generally moving about. Of all the shapes, the "dome" seems to be the most popular.

Once erected, these tents can be picked up and moved easily. This is handy if the wind changes and you want to face in a different direction. In heavy rain or under a blazing tropical sun (prolonged ultraviolet light can damage the material) the tent may then be carried and placed underneath a tarp for added protection. When striking camp, you can pick your tent up and shake out all the twigs, dead insects, and the watch you couldn't find!

Remember that these tents rely for their shape on *thin, flexible poles*. There is debate over whether these tents are as robust in high winds as the *rigid pole* mountain type. In stormy weather, flexible poles can bend alarmingly and even snap. If you intend to paddle in areas where there is an ever-present threat of storm-force winds, check the specifications of your tent and make sure that yours is designed to stand up to the conditions you might encounter.

Some freestanding tents are designed so that the fly sheet is supported by external poles. In wet weather, the inner tent can be set up dry under the protection of a fly sheet that is already standing in position.

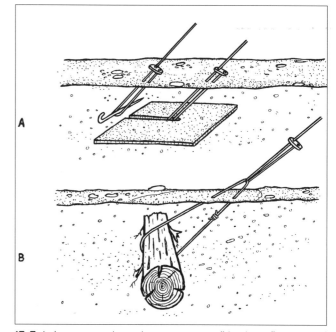

13-3. In loose ground, sand, or snow, use a "dead man" instead of a tent peg. A 6-by-6-inch piece of plywood or aluminum works well (A). A cord loop around a buried log (B) lessens friction and makes it easier to adjust the guy lines.

For Your Added Camping Comfort

Some tents have vestibules which can be purchased separately. This is a good, worthwhile investment.

Make sure that *all* seams of your tent have been sealed in the factory. A sealant from any good outdoor store should be used to waterproof any seams or any corners that have been missed.

Include some extra-long storm pegs to supplement the small, thin ones supplied with your tent. Make some snow/sand plates for your storm guys, from aluminum, plastic or plywood (see fig. 13-3).

Make a ground cloth out of waterproof material about an inch smaller than the size of your tent so that rain does not run down the tent, onto the ground cloth, and then under the tent floor. This goes between your tent and the ground to protect the thin, sewn-in ground sheet supplied with your tent. A few perforations here and there will allow rain water to drain out from between the tent and the ground cloth. After all, the cloth is there to prevent damage from the ground surface. It is not there to keep the bottom dry. An *internal* ground cloth is also a good idea, to prevent wear and tear on the inside of the tent.

If yours is a freestanding tent, take along a couple of those thin, flexible poles as spares. I learned my lesson after seeing a freestanding tent destroyed on the first night of a month-long wilderness expedition, as hurricane-force winds smashed its fiberglass poles to pieces and tore its fabric.

The Wonderful Tarp

Looking back over my camping career, I can remember so well those wretched hours spent huddled in a tent while the rain poured down. Sometimes I would be alone, while on other occasions I would accumulate bed sores while sharing my imprisonment with someone possessed of limited conversational skills. I would devour everything readable and still it would seem the rain would never stop. Sometimes one would hear the nearby snores from some lucky paddler who had been able to fall into a bored sleep. Rain effectively brought an end to any kind of social life.

And then I went to America and discovered the tarp.

I landed with a group late one overcast afternoon. The coastal forest was shrouded in mist. It was obvious that a downpour was due at any time, and I tried to prepare myself for a miserable evening. While I pitched my tent, however, I noticed a flurry of activity where I knew the kitchen area was going to be. When I finally got over there, I saw that a large square of tarpaulin had been slung, slightly at an angle, between some conveniently spaced trees. Nearby and almost touching the first one, a couple of other smaller tarps had been strung into position using paddles for support.

Then it started to rain.

It was like a miracle. No one seemed to take any notice of the downpour. Certainly no folks immediately darted for their tents. People congregated under the shelter, laughing. Conversation flourished and our cook prepared our evening meal completely unconcerned over the rain. We ate together under the tarp, and together we sat on

13-4. The wonderful tarp

logs and talked in the glow of the fire. The rain continued gently and no one cared.

Why, I wondered, had no one ever thought of the 10 feet x 10 feet or 15 feet x 15 feet tarp back in Britain? And why did I have to travel nearly 6,000 miles to discover the obvious?

The origins of the tarp shelter, it seems, date back to the days of the wagon trains. As they crawled slowly across an inhospitable continent, these prairie schooners were battered by all that the four seasons could throw at them. It was the heavy sailmaker's tarpaulins that shielded the precious cargoes of the early pioneers, and that were also utilized to make temporary shelters. Today's tarps can be made of any lightweight waterproof material, with plenty of eyelets around the edges.

Besides the social benefits, as a piece of survival equipment, your tarp could have many uses:

- It can be used as a stretcher to carry an injured person.
- It can haul or carry your equipment from the water's edge to your campsite—all in one go.
- It will collect rain water.
- You can sit in it and have a bath.
- It can be used as an animal trap.
- It will serve as a jury-rig sail.
- It will line a snow shelter.
- If you carry a sailmaker's palm in your repair kit, as I do for spray skirt repairs, you can be more ambitious. With patience and time on your hands, you could even use your tarp to cover a makeshift canoe frame. Remember, "necessity is the mother of invention."

Where to Make Camp

You have to be able to land in order to pitch a tent with any kind of success, so before you paddle off into the blue, get as much information as you can from the necessary chart and/or typographical map. More thought has to be given to landing when you have a fully loaded kayak. Sliding over a few weed-covered rocks in small surf, as you might do with an empty kayak, is not going to work with a fully loaded boat, so if possible look for sheltered beaches.

Campsites that would be ideal in some parts of the world would be just the opposite in others. For instance, in general, a good place to pitch camp would be in a sheltered spot at the mouth of a small freshwater stream. In bear country, however, this could be the worst possible place. When looking for a campsite, therefore, try to consider *everything*. The key word is *check*. Check the tides. You do not want to land at low water late in the evening, with half a mile of soft sand between you and that flat grassy knoll. Check to see if there are any restrictions to your landing en route—let alone camping. If possible check with paddlers who have been where you are going or who live there. Read everything about the area you can get your hands on.

Once you have landed successfully, look for somewhere that is sheltered from the wind. In mosquito country you might want to make life more pleasant by finding a spot that gets a slight breeze. Check the site first and make sure the ground where you are going to put your tent is flat and free from sharp stones and anything else that can poke a hole through your ground sheet. If you must sleep on sloping ground, sleep with your head higher than your feet; otherwise, you will wake up with a headache. A hollow will protect you from high winds but in wet weather it may revert to a pond. It is always nice to pitch your tent on flat, soft sand, but check the various high tide marks and use snow/sand plates to secure your guy lines. Camping areas administered by the U.S. Parks Service often have wooden platforms or lean-tos in which to pitch your tent. In some places, such as the Maine Island Trail, these platforms are in the form of a three-sided roofed shelter. You can either pitch your tent or sleep "in the open" on the wooden floor. In Florida's Everglades the Parks Service provides raised platforms called "chickees" that give paddlers a safe haven and a solid place to pitch their tents well above the indigenous alligator population.

If you have a choice, try to pitch your tent as near to your kayak as possible. This can save a lot of tiring journeys hauling all your miscellaneous equipment to and from the campsite. To cut down on walking trips, I have a very large bag that can carry four stowage bags at a time as well as lots of those little items that are awkward to carry.

Before settling down for the night, make sure your boat is pulled *well above the high water mark.* If in any doubt, tie your kayak to a tree or rock. If you are expecting to sit out a stormy night, kayaks and paddles can blow away, so stake them down.

Always be prepared for the worst. Even if you pitch your tent on a windless evening, always peg it down with long stakes and storm guys. For the time it takes it is well worth the peace of mind it gives. When the storm breaks in the middle of the night, you can lie in bed and listen to the others as they frantically run around in the wind and the rain, trying to keep their tents on the ground.

13-5. Alistaire Wilson, Tom Caskey, and Chris Jowsey make preparations for leaving Heather Island, near Alaska's Columbia Glacier.

PLANNING A TRIP

A journey can be planned as much as a year ahead of time with the help of tide tables, charts, and a *Tidal Stream Atlas*. The prevailing conditions, however, determine whether the trip will go ahead as planned.

It is incumbent on paddlers to acquaint themselves with local meteorological conditions that might cause sudden changes in the weather. It is also important to be able to interpret any weather information that appears in the press or on the radio and television. A small radio permanently tuned to continuous weather forecasts can be a priceless piece of equipment.

The most accurate weather forecasts are good only up to six hours or so. The immediate difference that an increase in wind strength or a change in the direction of the tide can make must always be foremost in one's mind.

The factor that governs the length of the trip and the degree of commitment possible is the strength and ability of the weakest member of the group.

At best the group will travel only at the speed of the slowest member. If the weather turns foul, a situation could occur that might easily get out of hand. Having to rescue inexperienced kayakers or having to tow them to safety places enormous burdens on the more experienced members of a party.

It is vital to know the coastline involved and apart from the necessary navigation and seamanship, it is also important to have an understanding of the subjects contained in this book. Remember that paddlers have been known to become very sick in their kayaks, to become affected by the sun's glare off the water, to become overheated or hypothermic, and to be taken ill. Never, therefore, undertake more than a simple journey with good escape routes in the company of untried, inexperienced paddlers who are unknown to you.

The average rate at which a small party of competent but inexperienced paddlers will travel is probably 2 knots plus the speed of the tidal stream. A strong head wind could drop this to 1 knot or less overall, and thus throw off your estimated time of arrival (ETA) and subsequent estimated time of departure (ETD). You must, therefore, appoint someone of sound judgment and someone who has an appreciation of the factors affecting sea journeys to remain on shore and serve as an emergency contact. If the need arises, this person can alert rescue services and save valuable time that the authorities might spend wondering whether or not you are really in trouble.

Preparing for Short Trips

If you are about to lead a group of eager kayakers on a sea trip—even a short one—the following checklist should run through your mind. Taking extra time at the beginning of a journey may save you a great deal of heartache later on. Take time to consider the following questions:

- Am I going far enough to merit informing the Coast Guard? If so, I will tell them: my name and qualifications; how many there are in the group; the type and color of our kayaks; what distress signals we carry; where we are going; the time we expect to return; any other relevant details.
- Are all the kayaks and spray covers serviceable and in good repair—no loose toggles or footrests?
- Are the boats full of flotation that will remain in them in the event of a capsize?
- Are the kits carried on the kayak decks fastened on tight?
- Who is carrying flares?
- Is everyone dressed adequately?
- Who looks the weakest?
- Does anyone have a special disability (such as deafness or diabetes)?
- Am I taking the group too far?
- Do I have enough help for what I intend to do with the group?
- Did I get a weather forecast?
- Have I taken the tides into consideration?
- Have I got all my own equipment?
- Did I lock the car?

During your deliberations, you may consider that one person in the group could put you all at risk. This might be due to the distance involved, the condition of the sea and weather, the state of his equipment, or some physical or psychological problems. If this is the case, he must be left behind. Be particularly careful in the case of some-one who has been recommended to you by someone else. Do not let feeling sorry for him or the persuasion of others deter you from a decision you feel is right and has the best interest of the group at heart.

When launching, involve your group in a study of the sequence and patterns of the oncoming waves so that they will become familiar with the driest and most efficient way of getting out through surf. Impress upon them the importance of keeping dry during extended expeditions that involve camping.

If the surf is dumping, the leader must leave the beach last. Launch the group one at a time. Hold each paddler steady at the water's edge so the wave will not sweep his boat sideways. As soon as there is a lull in the oncoming waves, push the boat off and out to sea. An outflowing rip will help considerably to get everyone clear of the beach.

Leading a Group

There should be no doubt about who the leader is. On the open sea, the ratio of leaders to students should be not fewer than one to eight. The leader should appoint a pathfinder to paddle out in front. If the conditions ahead are questionable or the route is uncertain, then the leader should go to the front. Under normal conditions, however, the leader will move about among the group offering advice and encouragement should anyone need it. Train your group to be aware of one another; show them how to twist their bodies around and turn their heads by trailing the back of their paddle blade on the water, thus looking right around on that side.

Members of a group should not paddle too far from one another. In rough seas and big swells, individuals can be hidden in the troughs. Some audible or visual signals such as a fog horn or a whistle should be agreed upon before the trip.

During rock-dodging or game-playing exercises close inshore, leaders should be careful not to let the members of their groups get behind rocks or into caves where they can be out of sight for more than a few minutes.

Do not take untried novices into situations where they have to cope with steep following seas a long way offshore until they have done simple forward running exercises close to the beach.

Landing

If you approach a beach where the surf is much larger than your group is used to, or, if the surf is dumping dangerously, stop well outside the surf line and explain to everyone what you intend to do and what you intend they should do to get ashore safely. Instruct the group to paddle in one at a time; then, if there is a capsize, you will only have one casualty to worry about. As they paddle in to shore, they must keep turning around and watching for any large waves approaching from behind. As soon as a wave reaches them, and if it is steep, the student should stop paddling or even back paddle if the wave is very large to prevent the kayak from surging forward and going out of control at surf speed. Once they have allowed the wave to pass under them, they must paddle fast again until the next wave catches up to them. As the paddlers reach shallow water where the waves are breaking, they must pause and wait for a lull in the big wave sets and then paddle in on the backs of smaller waves. Appoint someone to take charge and keep an eye on things while you go ashore first and land. The individuals can then be guided in one at a time with the help of some pre-arranged signals such as "Take care, wave behind," "Slow down," "Paddle fast." Once a boat reaches the beach, grab the toggle quickly and pull the paddler to safety.

Coping with Incidents

When a boat needs repair or there is a capsize, all paddlers should face the oncoming waves and hold their position close to the action without knocking into one another or impeding those involved in sorting out the problem. There will be a tendency for someone to start paddling off, and the rest will follow. It is vital that the leader keep this from happening. Therefore, it is better that the leader is not committed to the rescue, repair, tow, or whatever it may be. There could be times when speed is of the essence, however, and this is when the leader must deal with the matter at hand while at the same time keeping a watchful eye on the rest of the group.

Rafting up the rest of the party in this situation is not a desirable practice. (A raft is formed when two or more paddlers bring their kayaks alongside and connect them together by placing their paddles across the foredecks and holding on to each other's boat.) The raft drifts more quickly than an individual kayak and much more quickly than someone in the water holding on to a boat. It is

14-1. An Aleut Sea II enters the Panrhyn-mawr overfall off the coast of North Wales. The tide is running from left to right. (Photo courtesy Howard Jeffs)

extremely difficult for the raft to be maintained in waves, and when it comes to splitting up and proceeding with the trip, there could be considerable danger of capsize.

If a situation gets so out of hand that help is needed and certain individual paddlers are in danger of capsizing, rafting up in pairs is a good way of containing matters until help arrives. If, however, it is obvious that everyone might finish up by being blown out to sea, it is better for the group to maintain a course that keeps them paddling into the waves with the kayaks angled slightly into the wind. By angling into the wind, the boats are pointing into the waves and are less likely to capsize. It is hoped that the group can get itself close enough to the shore for the situation to be resolved.

The different effects of tide and wind should be noted. When the wind is against the tide, paddled kayaks or kayaks floating empty and high on the surface are more affected by the wind unless the tidal stream is very strong and the wind very light. Anyone in the water or a waterlogged kayak will move in the direction of the tidal stream, regardless of the strength of the wind. When the wind is blowing across the tidal stream, anyone in the water or a waterlogged boat will move in the direction of the tide with some pull by wind and wave action.

Planning an Expedition

Today there are not many corners of the globe left unexplored—perhaps "unspoiled" would be a better word. The kayak has certain highly specialized qualities, and it is the unique features of this craft that enable us to rediscover the world in which we live. Even familiar and well-trodden coastlines are giving up secrets to the inquisitive paddler. Expeditions led by kayak, therefore, may be to areas where others have been before, but the paddler is permitted to view the coastline from a different angle.

From a kayak one does truly see the world from a different angle. I remember gazing up at some sea cliffs in Baja California. There was a strata of volcanic ash that held the contents of some prehistoric seabed. The multitude of shells within this layer were still intact; the pressures of time had not yet turned these mollusks into fossils. It was as if I were watching history in the making. I felt a little smug as I thought that no craft other than a kayak would have been able to get close enough to shore to see this phenomenon, and that it would have been completely invisible to anyone walking along the top of the cliff.

It is sometimes difficult to decide which aspect of an expedition gives the most satisfaction—the actual paddling or the planning and preparations that take place during the months (sometimes years) beforehand. A tremendous amount of preparation goes into a comparatively small expedition, so allow at least one year to prepare any expedition in a foreign country. This preparatory stage is known as doing your homework, and for a start it means reading every book you can lay your hands on that contains information on the area you intend to visit. It is often a good idea to delegate certain areas of preparatory study to different members of the group. You will need to know all there is to know about the local weather, the people, the coastline, the topography of the area, what you can eat, and what will eat you. If the locals do not speak English, it might be worthwhile either to write down or learn a few phrases that might come in handy.

Letters will have to be written for advice, and it is certainly no good being proud. The best people to contact are explorers, scientists, mountaineers, or kayakers who have been to the area you intend to visit or one with similar conditions. Local information can be had from the local airlines or bush pilots, Coast Guard or similar organization, and the

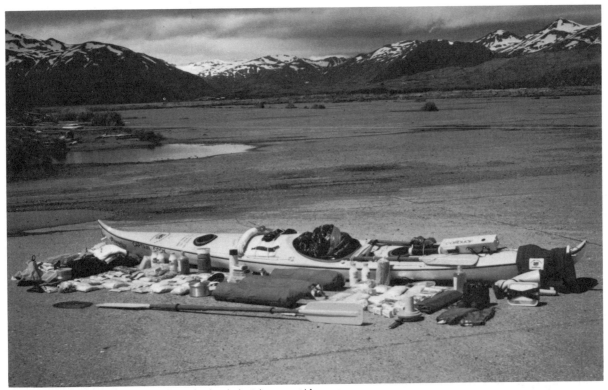

14-2. A Baidarka Explorer is ready to be loaded with a month's supply of equipment.

public information service in the foreign embassy of the country you intend to visit. If you make a bona fide inquiry, you will find the armed forces quite forthcoming with information.

Promoting the Expedition

If you expect to ask for sponsorship from firms or individuals, you should send them an outline of your proposed expedition and a personal letter. The outline of your expedition should include:

- The inclusive dates.
- A list of the members and their qualifications, their functions on the expedition, and any previous experience.
- The locality, with a map and insets to show specific locations.
- A brief outline of your aims and objectives (whether photographic, scientific, sporting, competitive).
- A background to the proposed expedition.
- Your plans versus what others have done in the past.
- The names of any supporting or sponsoring scientific bodies.
- Your plans for any specimens you bring back.
- How you will reward individual sponsors (e.g., either by publishing photographs of you using their product or including their name on photographs used by others).

You must satisfy the needs of sponsors so that any expeditions following in your footsteps will not be rebuffed when they apply for assistance.

Calculating Costs

You must be realistic and up-to-date with your expenses. There will be the cost of duplicating and postage so that your handout can be distributed. Air fares, overland transport, hire of vehicles or charter planes must be considered. In some parts of the world it may be necessary to hire porters. The price of fuel and consequently the cost of some kinds of transportation vary greatly in different parts of the world. Insurance will be necessary for yourselves and the kayaks. The kayaks may also have to be packaged and stored. You may have to subsist in civilization while waiting for any unexpected contingencies (weather, repairs, or boats delayed by customs).

The type of food to be carried must be decided upon (dehydrated or freeze-dried). Is it to be ordered abroad and delivered to your launching base or is it to be transported from the expedition's country of origin? Special equipment to be considered includes distress radios or beacons, cameras and film, medical supplies, firearms, and ammunition. Finally, the cost of publishing an expedition report at the end of the trip has to be considered.

Choosing Companions

Choosing the right people for a kayak expedition into wilderness areas can be crucial to the success of your venture. Constraints of time and money may force incompatible paddlers together. It often comes as a shock when paddlers with a common interest in sea kayaking find they have nothing else in common. Long-standing friends may become unrecognizable to each other when confronted with the stress of an arduous trip or the challenges of a hostile environment.

Personality clashes can mean the failure of an expedition. It is essential, therefore, to assess each member of your expedition as thoroughly as possible. Probably the best way to do this is to spend as much time as possible paddling together before the trip.

Coping with Dissension

In a wilderness situation, the battle against fatigue, anxiety, and the elements can be very one-sided, particularly when loneliness has to be faced as a result of character clashes, dissension, petty recriminations, and jealousies generated in small groups formed among expedition members.

Although cliques are obviously undesirable in any situation, they are more easily absorbed—and may sometimes even go unnoticed—if the expedition is a large one. With small kayak expeditions, however, cliques or minority factions can jeopardize the success of the whole venture.

In a survival situation demoralization makes individuals easy prey to exposure. Any clique that excludes a minority can cause the smaller group to fight for survival in no uncertain terms. Loneliness can do strange things: It either brings individuals to the verge of collapse, or it forces them to rely on one another for protection and comfort. It is while drawing upon that inner strength while the chance of survival is slipping out of his own hands, that a man may place himself in the hands of God.

Loneliness, anxiety, doubt, fear, despair, and apprehension are all nails in the coffin of survival, and in this kind of situation, one's companions can be a deciding factor in the battle to survive. A person who has trustworthy companions and true friends can overcome fear; even death can be faced with calmness and fortitude if the comfort that friendship can bring is at hand.

Importance of a Leader

Before considering what qualities a leader should possess, we might question why there should be a leader at all. First, it is important that there is one individual who can act and speak for the expedition as a whole because with special status this person will be more able to negotiate with such people as customs agents or foreign embassies. If your expedition is one of special merit, it may be necessary to meet and bargain with film or television companies, and once again it is better to leave negotiations to one person. A well-known and respected person who is designated leader can give credulity to a scheme that at first glance might seem impossible to the uninitiated public. Sponsors are happier if they know that someone is responsible for fulfilling the expedition's promises of photographs and publicity articles that show their products in an interesting or exciting manner.

Someone must also be able to take the responsibility if or when things start to go wrong; these problems can range from missing items of equipment to serious injury or loss of life.

It would be ridiculous for any one person to try to do all the organizing jobs alone. For that reason the leader will have to spread the load and delegate some of the jobs. By knowing the group well, the leader is in the best position to allocate tasks to those members of the group who are best suited to undertake them. In this way jobs will not be duplicated during the more hectic stages of preparation.

Good leaders should be diplomatic, and all major problems should be discussed by the whole group, although the final decision should be with the person who takes overall responsibility. Regardless of personality, there must be something about the leader that inspires the confidence and trust of others.

No matter how democratic the discussions have been in planning, preparation, and initial stages of the expedition, inevitably there will be a time when a decision must be made with no time for discussion or debate. At such a time the leader must feel able to make this decision and others must have sufficient trust to abide by it.

Because the decisions of the leader could affect the lives of every member of the expedition, the person who leads must be the master of the kayaking craft in the broadest sense of the word. This does not necessarily mean that the leader should be the strongest or the most skillful. The leader's competence and vast experience, however, should inspire confidence in any decision he makes, especially with regard to the navigational and safety aspects of the expedition.

The leader should be sensitive to any problems or discomfort suffered by the group as a whole or any individual member who has a specific physical or psychological problem during the trip or even during the preparatory stages before the expedition sets off.

A good leader should be farsighted enough to anticipate problems before they occur. For example, in cases of friction between members of the group, the leader should act as a calming influence and serve as a mediator.

Because the alternative to crying is often laughing, expedition leaders would be well advised to cultivate their sense of humor. Many an expedition has been held together by a good laugh when everything seems to have gone miserably wrong.

Far-Reaching Responsibilities

As an ocean kayaker you can be considered more than just a sportsman once you become competent. With advanced skills and good equipment, you are a highly trained operative who has the facility to offer help and relief to many people in different ways.

Your kayak can assist in rescues impossible for other craft because it can pick its way through drifting ice or floating logs. Its shallow draft also

14-3. The author is carrying a month's supply of food and equipment in his kayak. What cannot be squeezed inside the boat has to be carried on the deck. In the background are Alaska's Chugach Mountains. (Photo courtesy Tom Caskey)

allows it to navigate close inshore over kelp beds where no other vessel would be able to go.

The distress flares that you have with you can be sent skyward on behalf of others, while the compass on your deck could help guide less prudent water users who are lost in thick fog.

You should be carrying a small but well-stocked first-aid kit. Then it would not be difficult for you to leave your kayak and board another small vessel to administer assistance should this become necessary.

Your repair kit can also be used on behalf of others. My pliers have cut fishhooks from the fingers of careless fishermen, and the repair tape has been used to bind up leaking fuel pipes. The life jacket or buoyancy aid you wear can be taken off and given to someone in greater need, perhaps someone already in distress in the water. If a small boat were to sink completely, quite a number of people could hang on around your gunwale and

be supported. This would have to be done evenly around the boat so that your stability would be maintained.

High winds do not blow kindly on small motorboats with engine failure, but a strong paddler can usually hold a small boat and prevent it from drifting onto rocks by using a towline.

Using the buoyancy of a kayak as support, assistance can be given to anyone trapped by extensive mud flats or quicksand.

To sum up, the presence of a calm, experienced, and well-equipped paddler in a craft as versatile and as seaworthy as today's ocean kayak should be a source of reassurance and an asset to all other water users.

Conclusion

I have tried in some way to prepare you for quite a few of the problems that may arise both on and off the water. I have no doubt, however, that on your travels you will make some brand new mistakes and encounter some brand new problems all your own—some perhaps of your own making. And like me, you will probably paddle the wrong boat in the wrong weather in the wrong place and with badly chosen companions. Like those who have paddled before you, you will learn by your mistakes, but whether you fight against screaming winds or glide serenely across a velvet carpet of early morning mist, revel in the mastery of your craft and enjoy every second.

So take your beautiful replica of the hunter's boat and rediscover the world—or perhaps just rediscover your world—in the sunshine and in the company of true friends. The ocean is all yours.

It is calm, the smooth sea heaves in a long swell towards the rocky islets that fringe the shore, a light haze still lies over the sounds between them, and the sea-birds floating on the surface seem double their natural size. The kaiaks cut their way forwards, side by side, making only a silent ripple; the paddles swing in an even rhythm, while the men keep up an unbroken stream of conversation, and now and then burst out into merry laughter. (Nansen, Eskimo Life, *pp. 59–60.)*

Appendix 1:
Sea Proficiency Test—Kayak

Examiner: BCU Senior Instructor (Sea) E1

Note: The purpose of this test is to ensure that the candidate has sufficient knowledge and skill to enable him or her to take a kayak safely to sea under a competent leader.

The test must be taken at sea, under moderate conditions (wind or sea state 2–4). Allowance will be made by the examiner if conditions are rough, but the kayak skills must be performed in a competent manner. For reasons of safety three kayaks will participate. The test will not be taken in a flat calm.

The candidate must have taken part in at least three 1-day expeditions at sea. To rate as a qualifying expedition, the journey must have been on open water—where it is *possible* to be three miles from land in any direction.

The journey may, however, be inshore, close to a simple coastline, not involving overfalls, tidal races, difficult landings, or open crossings. Winds not exceeding Force 4. Not more than one trip shall be carried out on an estuary. The journey must have involved four hours traveling, with a lunch break in which the candidate was self-sufficient for food and drink. At least one journey must be on an entirely different stretch of coast to the other two.

The controlling wrist must be used to position the paddle blade for all strokes.

The candidate will:

1. Present him- or herself suitably equipped for the test. Borrowed equipment will be judged as though it was the candidate's own.
2. Present for inspection the following items, which must be both suitable and serviceable:

(a) *Kayak, paddle, and spray cover. Spray cover must be fitted with efficient release strap.
(b) Kayaks must be provided with end grabs suitable for carrying out rescues without trapping the hand.
(c) Safety lines and/or painters (if fitted) must be taut and not capable of becoming loose accidentally, or fouling the cockpit area.
(d) Buoyancy, a minimum of 12.5 kgs (30 lbs) at each end. Buoyancy must be securely fixed. Examiners may require buoyancy to fill all available space apart from cockpit.
(e) Buoyancy aid or Lifejacket. Minimum 6 kgs inherent buoyancy.
(f) Repair kit and simple first-aid kit.
(g) Rudder and steering gear if fitted.
(h) Adequate spare clothing, applicable to the prevailing conditions, and suitable for use in an exposure bag to prevent hypothermia.
(i) Waterproof kitbag(s). The equipment must be carried in the kitbag(s) for the test and must remain dry. The examiner may well fail a candidate whose kit becomes unduly wet following a capsize.
(j) Windproof anorak, ideally with hood. Brightly coloured crash helmet and/or woolly hat is recommended.
(k) Simple compass.

*The test may be taken in any suitable kayak, provided it is equipped and safe for sea touring purposes.

3. Pack the waterproof kitbag(s) with the neces-

sary items for a day's tour and stow it (them) in the boat. The bag(s) must remain fixed in during capsize. In addition to the items listed at 2 above, the following will be included:
(a) packed lunch; (b) equipment for providing a hot drink (may be a vacuum flask); (c) emergency food; (d) flares or other suitable means of indicating distress; (e) whistle; (f) exposure bag of minimum size 6' by 3'.
The following items are also recommended:
(a) equipment for making a hot drink; (b) torch; (c) matches or lighter.

4. Tie the following knots: Bowline, Figure of eight, Round turn and two half hitches, Clove hitch.

5. Demonstrate:
   (a) Launching and embarking. The boat must be floating. Balance must be maintained. The paddle must remain within reach. If paddle is used for support, the hands should not hold the loom outside of the gunnels. Paddle at least 50m offshore into deep water—well out of depth.
   (b) Efficient paddling technique, forwards and backwards. The examiner will look for: correct dynamic seating position; correct entry and exit of the blade; ability to keep the boat straight; sufficient power in the stroke to paddle against wind or current; trunk rotation; correct width of paddle grip.
   (c) Turning the kayak 360 degrees in both directions by using alternate forward and reverse sweep strokes. Paddle blade just covered, reaching out to full arm extension, elbow slightly bent. Paddle drawing well into the stern with the forward arm pushing across the body. Body turning to place the paddle in the water at the stern of the kayak. If fitted with a rudder, the kayak must be turned again in both directions, this time steering with rudder only.
   (d) Emergency stops, forwards and backwards. Reverse direction should be in evidence within 4 strokes.
   (e) Drawing the kayak sideways in both directions. Top arm high, blade deep. The boat must keep a straight line sideways through the water in both directions.
   (f) High and low recovery strokes to be performed on both sides. For high braces the water must reach the paddler's waist, with a strong pull and associated hip flick to recover.
   (g) Paddle brace, high and low on the left and right. Where wave conditions are not suitable, the candidate must paddle hard forwards then glide with the blade flat on the surface at right angles to the kayak.
      For a high brace, the water must reach the paddler's waist at the onset of the stroke.
   (h) Stern rudder. The paddle blade should be placed in the water upright, well back to the stern. Candidate should be able to keep the kayak running straight, down wind on small waves, with the paddle kept on one side of the boat.

6. Demonstrate:
   (a) Bringing the kayak alongside a jetty or another kayak. The boat must point up-wind or up-tide, whichever is the stronger.
   (b) Bringing the kayak into a beach forwards, sideways and backwards (forwards only if kayak is fitted with rudder). This is controlled, not a "surf" landing. Holding position in order to allow for the waves.

7. Perform capsize drill, followed by a deep water rescue with partners. Take charge of a rescue and then act as a capsized patient. Any sign at all of fear or panic, and failure to retain the kayak during the drill will automatically result in failure of the test. The capsize must

be "accidental" with spray deck in place—either while paddling or in an attempted recovery stroke or sculling for support.

8. Prove that he or she can swim. Swim 50 metres in canoeing clothing (wet or dry suits are permitted) and a buoyancy aid or life-jacket. In the last 10 metres of the swim the lifejacket, if worn, must be inflated.

9. Answer questions on:
(a) Practical experience, giving firm evidence of having taken part in at least 3 one-day expeditions at sea; (b) Safety precautions applying particularly to the kayak at sea; (c) The general effects of tide, current and wind; (d) Local Coast Guard organization and rescue services; (e) Local waters and conditions; (f) Recognizing hazards, estimating tidal speeds and directions, and understanding depths and drying heights, all from a chart.

10. Show that he or she can do simple tidal predictions by the tidal constant method.

11. Demonstrate an ability to use a simple compass to follow an escape route.

12. Demonstrate an elementary knowledge of first aid: How to stop bleeding; what to do for a broken bone; how to treat an unconscious, breathing patient.

Appendix 2:
Advanced Proficiency Test— Sea Kayak

Administered by the National Coaching Committee of the BCU, these tests have been devised to encourage the correct and safe handling of kayaks in advanced touring situations.

This leaflet deals only with the ADVANCED SEA KAYAK PROFICIENCY test, which may be taken in a sea kayak or a suitable kayak fitted out for sea touring.

Those who are successful will receive the appropriate certificate. Holders of the Advanced Proficiency Test certificate will be entitled to buy a silver lapel badge.

A kayak paddler who has qualified for the silver badge in both kayak (inland and sea tests) and the Canoe Advanced test is entitled to wear the BCU gold badge.

The 4 and 5 STAR tests are concerned with handling skills only. Sea leaflet ST3.

Entry Details

1 It is NOT necessary to attend a prior training course for Advanced Proficiency Tests, although these are available throughout the country, and are recommended.
2 Advanced tests may only be taken at specially staged assessment sessions, examined by a BCU Coach (or grade III examiner). Available courses are arranged nationally in the calendar which is sent free to all members. Further details are available on request to the BCU office.
3 A paddler may not enter for the Advanced test until he or she has been successful in the equivalent Proficiency test in the same type of craft.
4 A properly maintained record MUST be produced by candidates for Advanced level tests.

Purpose of the Test

The purpose of this test is to ensure that the successful candidate has sufficient knowledge and skill to lead others of similar ability on advanced sea journeys with safety in British spring, summer and autumn conditions.

Previous Experience

The candidate must give evidence (log book, etc.) that his experience includes six advanced day trips in at least two different sea areas. The candidate must have assisted the leader in the planning of at least three of these trips.

The following experience/conditions must have been met at some stage either during the six journeys or on additional excursions.

1. A journey of minimum distance 20 nautical miles.
2. An open crossing of at least 7 nautical miles, 1 mile of which must have been at least 3 miles away from land.
3. Navigation in poor visibility or darkness.
4. Tidal streams of at least 3 knots.
5. Winds reaching at least Force 4.
6. Exposure to no-landing zones.
7. Paddling on tide races or overfalls.
8. Camping from a kayak on a sea journey.
9. Handling and rescuing laden kayaks.

Practical Test

Any suitable kayak may be used for the test. The advanced paddler may often find him- or herself leading groups who themselves paddle sea kayaks, so experience of sea kayaks is an advantage. It is not a prerequisite.

The candidate will pack the kayak with suitable equipment for an overnight camp/bivvi, in preparation for a two-day journey. The test will be carried out with kayaks thus loaded and may include an overnight camp. The candidate must be prepared for the paddling to continue into hours of darkness and must be able to navigate his or her kayak during hours of darkness. He or she must be prepared to deal with likely emergency situations.

Flares must be easily accessible, and the candidate must be conversant with procedures for firing.

The candidate must demonstrate ability to keep a compass course on open water and make good a course across a tide stream using transits. He or she must demonstrate an ability to take bearings on known features.

Candidate must demonstrate an ability to plan from a chart an alternative route to a safe landing while afloat on a journey in the event of a change in weather or emergency, taking into consideration the tide stream.

He or she must demonstrate an ability to handle the kayak competently in 3–5 foot surf, including maneuvering on waves forwards, backwards, and sideways and rolling under breaking waves. This part of the test may be carried out in suitable overfalls or tide races.

The candidate must demonstrate an ability to effect successful landings and launchings in a variety of situations.

The following skills must be demonstrated in an area of choppy water, as these are the conditions in which they are most likely to be needed.

1. Capsize and exit from kayak followed by a successful solo re-entry and retreat to calmer area for empty out. (Rafted assistance may be given while emptying kayak).
2. Demonstrate and take charge of, with partners, a deep water rescue.
3. Demonstrate an Eskimo roll after capsize to both left and right.
4. Tow a capsized victim and kayak from an area of disturbed water into a calmer area for a rescue.

While afloat the candidate must demonstrate his ability to cope with problems of the following kind:
1. Repairing a holed kayak.
2. Towing an incapacitated person (e.g., with dislocated shoulder).
3. Safely landing an injured paddler.
4. Demonstrate approved method of resuscitation.
5. Produce spare paddlers.
6. Produce whistle, emergency food.

Theory

Answer questions on the following with the aid of a chart where necessary.
a) Repairs and maintenance.
b) The causes of tides and tidal streams and how to allow for them, and the cause and effect of clapotis.
c) Sea conditions and the effects of wind particularly on:
   1) Shelving bottoms.
   2) Lea shore.
   3) Rips.
   4) Overfalls.
   5) Tide races.
d) Weather forecasting from observation of cloud formation, e.g., recognizing approaching fronts and line squalls, and the means of obtaining and understanding weather forecasts.
e) Group leadership and control.
f) Estuary canoeing to include buoyage, understanding of chart symbols, light and sound signals, particular dangers such as moorings, moorings in tideways, and movement of shipping.

g) Types of kayak and equipment applicable to the sea.

h) Hypo- and Hyperthermia—what to look for, how to avoid, and the treatment.

Chartwork

Plan an advanced sea journey using an unfamiliar chart, pilot, *tide stream atlas* and tide tables. A weather forecast will be given which may take the form of a shipping forecast.

The prepared journey should be summarized to an extent that it may be simply explained to a group as instructions for a day's paddle. Instructions should include information such as:

1) Compass bearings and times estimated for crossings and allowances made for wind.
2) General direction of tidal stream.
3) Places where conditions are likely to be rough.
4) Useful transits for gauging progress.
5) Departure time and ETA. at appropriate points.
6) Sound signals/fog horns audible if bad visibility is likely.
7) Lights visible and their position if paddling extends into hours of darkness.
8) Estimated paddling speed.
9) Information for base contact.

The chartwork exercise is normally expected to take two hours.

Appendix 3:
Senior Instructor Assessment

Essential Information for Candidates

The purpose of the award is to provide a minimum qualification for a person to be in charge of kayaking activities for a club or school, which includes expeditioning and/or white-water grade II, or equivalent sea conditions (as appropriate).

It is assumed that a Senior Instructor will work within his or her personal capabilities, but that as knowledge and experience increases, he or she will become capable of leading on more difficult grades of water. The relevant Advanced Proficiency Certificate is a useful endorsement for this purpose.

The Assessment is based on:
1. Test of kayaking abilities.
2. Test of practical teaching abilities.
3. Test of practical group control and expedition leadership abilities, including safety provision and first aid.
4. Test of theoretical expedition leadership abilities, general knowledge, and an ability to impart knowledge in a class situation.

Essential information for all Senior Instructor Assessment candidates:

Have You—

Obtained your COCLG Assistant Lifeguard Award or RLSS Bronze Medallion?

An up-to-date log book with evidence of 50 hours relevant instruction—please ensure that entries are complete.

Current full individual membership of BCU or National Association? Card must be brought to the assessment. (Comprehensive and Comprehensive Family and Youth categories count as full individual membership but *not* Basic categories. An adjustment will be made by the BCU office for those needing to convert from Basic category to comprehensive (or full) membership.)

Completed all details on the Award Entry Form, including name and address of invigilator for your written paper? Please return form in advance, together with assessment fee.

Evidence of attendance at relevant Training Course?

Personal clothing and kayak equipped in accordance with the requirements of the relevant proficiency test? This *must* be brought to the assessment, together with the specific items listed:

Repair kit capable of repairing a large hole in wet conditions; first-aid kit; tow line; spare split paddles; adequate spare clothing, applicable to the prevailing conditions, and suitable for use in an exposure bag to prevent hypothermia; waterproof container(s); vacuum flask and equipment for making a hot drink; whistle; exposure bag (min. 6' X 3'); torch; matches or lighter; spare paddles. Inland—line and float; Sea—flares (1 red parachute and 1 hand-held red flare is minimum) and compass (Orienteering type is sufficient).

Personal Ability and Leadership Requirements

Personal Performance

The candidate must be able to perform to a reasonable level the skills defined in the 1–3 Star Tests, and the Proficiency Test, and be able to handle him- or herself competently on grade II water (inland) or in moderate conditions (winds up to Force 4) on the open sea, and handle 2'–3' surf.

It is highly desirable that a Senior Instructor be able to roll. While it is not *in itself* a fail factor for Senior Instructor assessment purposes, those not able to demonstrate reasonable beginnings in the skill will need to compensate by satisfying the examiners very fully as to their general kayaking ability.

Group Control

This is assessed during practical teaching and expedition leadership sessions. It involves the candidate's ability to:
1. Ensure the safety of the group.
2. Maintain interest.
3. Demonstrate awareness of the environment.

Practical Teaching

The candidate must be able to demonstrate, analyze, and teach effectively the 1–3 Star and Proficiency Test skills. He or she must also be able to spot obvious errors, and correct them.

Rescues and Towing Techniques

A competent performance of the main deep-water rescues is required, relevant to the award (i.e., Sea or Inland). White-water rescues should include piggy-backing the swimmer ashore and nudging kayak to bank.

A quick-release method must be incorporated in both body-anchored and boat-anchored systems. Candidates must be aware of the necessity to take the whole situation into account.

Throw-line systems should be capable of reaching 15 meters. Inland Candidates must have knowledge of where to place protection, where to aim the line, how to "play" the swimmer into an eddy, and the importance of belay.

Lecturettes

Your lecturette topic will be notified in advance. Candidates should keep strictly to their allotted 10 minutes. Time will be allowed for discussion and comment.

Expedition Planning

Candidates must demonstrate:
Planning of journey suitable for stated category of group.
Knowledge of how to obtain information concerning route.
Use of Ordinance Survey (OS) map.
Ability to identify possible hazards en route.
Ability to make suitable transport arrangements.
Allowance for "escape" routes.
Ability to advise candidates on suitable equipment and clothing.
Sea Candidates must be able to plan a coastal or estuary expedition using linear measurement only.

Expedition Leadership

The assessors will look for:
1. Prior planning and thought.
2. Group equipment check.
3. Safety and control. Were the potential hazards spotted? Was the instructor in the right place at the right time?
4. Use of teaching situations which may naturally occur.
5. Group enjoyment.
6. Dealing with emergencies, real or contrived by the assessors.
7. Ability to paddle efficiently against current or wind.

Oral Examination

The candidate's general knowledge and attitude will be assessed.

Inspection of Equipment

Equipment should conform to requirements.

First Aid and Lifesaving

Please note that where the lifesaving test has been taken more than five years previously, examiners may require a practical demonstration of the relevant skills during an assessment course.

The following questions require a correct answer:

How would you stop severe bleeding?

What would you do if someone broke their arm or leg?

How would you treat an unconscious, breathing patient.

Re-Assessment

Please note that should you not be successful in passing the Senior Instructor assessment, a minimum period of three months must elapse before attending a further assessment course.

A Warning About the British Canoe Union's Instructor Award

The purpose of the award is to provide a qualification for those wishing to introduce others to kayaking on simple waters only. The Instructor award is *not* regarded as being of sufficiently high standard for the safe supervision of kayaking activities on the open sea. It is aimed at a much lower level than the Senior Instructor award, and is directed toward those who show a disinclination to rough water kayaking and/or rolling skills.

The Instructor award is not an expedition leadership award. There is therefore no such thing as a "Sea Instructor."

Index

Boldface numerals indicate pages on which photographs or illustrations appear.